5

Mathemagic

Mathemagic

The 1978 Childcraft Annual

An annual supplement to
Childcraft—The How and Why Library

World Book–Childcraft International, Inc.

A subsidiary of Field Enterprises, Inc.

Chicago London Paris Rome Sydney Tokyo Toronto

Acknowledgments

The publishers of *Childcraft—The How and Why
Library* gratefully acknowledge the courtesy of
the following publishers, agencies, authors, and
organizations for permission to use copyrighted
stories, poems, and illustrations in this volume.
Full illustration acknowledgments appear on
page 298.

National Council of Teachers of Mathematics:
"The Roads of Math" by Jeffrey Dielle, reprinted
from the *Arithmetic Teacher,* October 1966 (vol.
13, p. 467), © 1966 by the National Council of
Teachers of Mathematics, used by permission.

Photograph of Stonehenge, page 254, © 1976
Georg Gerster, Photo Researchers, Inc.

Random House, Inc.: "Milo in Digitopolis"
condensed by permission of Random House, Inc.,
from *The Phantom Tollbooth* by Norton Juster,
copyright © 1961 by Norton Juster, courtesy
Wm. Collins Sons & Co. Ltd.

Paul R. Reynolds, Inc.: "Tuesday I Was Ten"
from *Don't Ever Cross a Crocodile* by Kaye
Starbird, copyright © 1963 by Kaye Starbird,
reprinted by permission of Paul R. Reynolds,
Inc., 599 Fifth Avenue, New York, N.Y. 10017.

Contents

Preface

Mathematics? Ick! Ugh!

That's the way most children—and many grown-ups—feel. The very word *mathematics* makes us think of pages of dreary number problems, rules that are hard to remember, and lots of things we just don't understand.

But you won't find anything of that sort in *this* book! For this is a book about the *magic* of math. It is filled with puzzles, tricks, games, surprises, stories, poems, and facts that show the magic hidden in numbers and shapes!

In this book you'll visit a strange land where the people are all shapes, such as squares, circles, triangles, and the like. You'll learn how to find the "magic number" in your name, and what it might mean. You'll learn how to make a marvelous counting machine that's really fun to play with. You'll discover some things that might help you have better "luck" in some of the games you play. And you'll learn how to do some tricks with a paper ring that will absolutely astound you!

But most important of all, you'll discover what mathematics is really all about. For there's a lot more to mathematics—or, as you will soon begin to think of it, *mathemagic*— than you ever suspected. It really is a lot of fun! But, of course, it takes work, too. Arithmetic may often seem hard and boring. But it's only a very small part of the whole, big world of mathematics. As you grow older, you'll find that mathematics is a kind of magic carpet. It will take you to places you never even dreamed of and help you to do all kinds of wonderful things.

1

Puzzle fun!

Do you like puzzles and "thinking games"?
Well, here are some for you.
So on with your thinking cap and see
Just how well you are able to do!

These pages of games and puzzles
Will give you some minutes of fun.
And after you've solved them you'll be surprised
To find out just *what* you have done!

The wolf, the goat, and the cabbages

More than a thousand years ago, a man wrote a book of puzzles—the kind of puzzles we call "brain teasers." Here is one of the puzzles from that book. See if you can solve it.

There was once a man who made his living by taking people and things across a river. But his boat was so small he could take only one person or thing at a time.

One day, the man was given three things to take across the river—a wolf, a goat, and a big basket of cabbages. Because he could take only one thing at a time, he would have to leave two things behind and come back for them. And that meant trouble!

If he took the cabbages and left the wolf and goat behind, the wolf would eat the goat! And if he took the wolf and left the goat with the cabbages, the goat would eat the cabbages!

Of course, he could take the goat across first, and leave the cabbages with the wolf, for the wolf would not eat them. But then what? He would have to bring either the wolf or the cabbages across the river on his second trip, and then *something* would be eaten while he went back for the last thing.

The man was sure there had to be a way to get the three things across the river, one at a time, without ever leaving the wolf and the goat, or the goat and the cabbages, together. And, after a while, he had the answer!

What do you think it was? He didn't tie up the wolf so it couldn't eat the goat. He didn't hang the sack of cabbages from a tree so the goat couldn't get them. He got the three things across the river one at a time—without ever leaving the wolf and goat, or the goat and the cabbages, together. See if you can figure out how he did it. If you can't, look on page 20 for the answer. But try to work out the puzzle first.

A moving numbers game

You can play this game by yourself, on the floor or on a table. You need only five playing cards—an ace, 2, 3, 4, and 5. Lay the cards out just as they are shown in the picture at the top of this page.

To play the game, you move the cards, one at a time, until you get all the numbers in the right order—the ace (1), 2, and 3 in the top row and the 4 and 5 in the bottom row. But you can't simply pick up a card and put it wherever you wish. You can only *slide* a card into an empty space that is next to it. For example, at the start of the game there is an empty space at the end of the bottom row. You can slide the 5 *down* or slide the 2 *across*. But you can't move any other card because no other card is next to the empty space.

After you move a card into an empty space, you'll then have a new empty space into which another card can be moved. Each time you slide a card into a space it counts as one move. It is possible to put all of the cards in order in only ten moves—but it may take you a lot more! Try the game out for a while. If you find you can't put the cards in order in ten moves, look on page 20 and see how it's done.

The magic word

There was once a very large, fat, and quite handsome bullfrog by the name of Ribidip, who lived in a small pond in a forest. He was well-liked by the mud turtles, was friends with most of the fish, and was on very good terms with all the birds.

However, there lived in the forest a very long, very terrifying black snake whose name was Sinister Hiss. And Ribidip lived in constant fear that one day he would meet Sinister Hiss and that would be the end of him. For snakes are very fond of frogs—but not as friends!

Now, in a big hollow tree in the forest there lived a wise old badger who was known far and wide as a magician. One day Ribidip went to see him, to ask if there was any way he could protect himself from Sinister Hiss. "Isn't there some kind of magic spell you can give me so that I can save myself?" he pleaded.

The badger thought for a while. Then, using ink made of berry juice, he wrote this magical code on a piece of birch bark:

0 1 2 3 4 5 6 7 8 9
E H M T Z A P S L P

"Now you must perform a magical spell," said the badger. "Write down any number that has three numerals, such as 265. But the first numeral and the last must have a difference of at least *two*—such as 2 and 5, or 6 and 8.

"Then, take the number you have written and turn it around so that the last numeral in it becomes the first. If your number was 265, you'd now write 562.

"Now you have two numbers. Subtract the smaller of the two numbers from the larger.

"Take your answer and turn *it* around, so that the last numeral becomes the first. Then add the turned-around number to the number that you got when you subtracted. This will give you four numerals. Each of the numerals stands for one of the letters in the magical code on the birch bark. These letters will make a magic word that you must shout out as loudly as you can if Sinister Hiss tries to eat you!"

What was the magic word Ribidip had to shout? Do as the Badger said and you'll find out!

If you can't work out the magic word, look on page 21 and see how it's done.

16

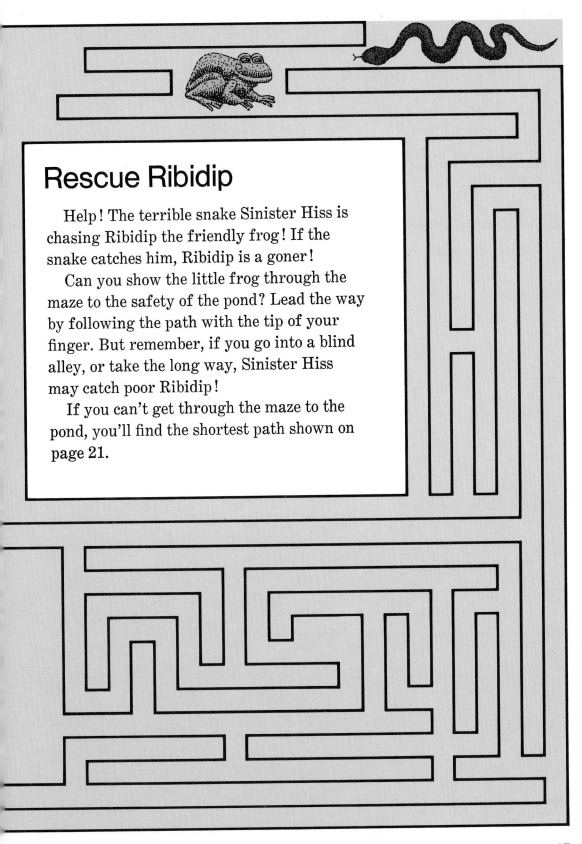

Rescue Ribidip

Help! The terrible snake Sinister Hiss is chasing Ribidip the friendly frog! If the snake catches him, Ribidip is a goner!

Can you show the little frog through the maze to the safety of the pond? Lead the way by following the path with the tip of your finger. But remember, if you go into a blind alley, or take the long way, Sinister Hiss may catch poor Ribidip!

If you can't get through the maze to the pond, you'll find the shortest path shown on page 21.

The mysterious and magical Möbius strip!

If you have a piece of paper, that paper will have two sides, right? If you wanted to, you could color one side red and the other side blue, couldn't you? And even if you roll the paper into a tube, it still has two sides—an inside and an outside.

But could you have a piece of paper that has only *one* side?

Well, let's see. Get a piece of paper and cut off a long, narrow strip. With a pencil, put an A at the left end of the strip, and a B at the right

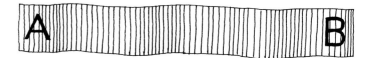

end. Now, turn the strip over, keeping the B on your right. Bring the two ends together. Next, twist the B end and place the B on top of the A. Tape the ends together with transparent tape. Put tape on both sides. Now you have a loop with a half twist in it.

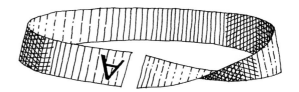

The loop looks as if it has two sides, doesn't it? If you had a *giant* loop, you and a friend could begin coloring each side—one side red and the other side blue. But if you did, you would be amazed to find that your colors would bump into each other! For this kind of loop actually

has only one side! Start coloring your small loop red and see for yourself.

This kind of twisted loop is called a Möbius strip, after the man who invented it. And it's a strange and almost "magical" sort of toy that you can do some surprising things with. For example, what do you think would happen if you were to cut a Möbius strip straight down the middle? Do you think you would get two loops? No, indeed! After you finish cutting it

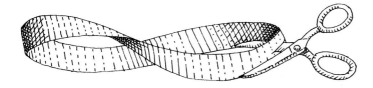

in "half," you'll find that you still have only *one* loop—but it is twice as long as the one you started with!

> *A mathematician confided*
> *That a Möbius strip is one-sided.*
> *And you'll get quite a laugh*
> *If you cut one in half*
> *For it stays in one piece when divided!*

What do you think would happen if you cut *that* loop down the middle? Well, try it and see!

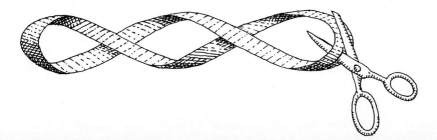

Guess what you've been doing!

Were you able to guide Ribidip through the maze to the safety of the pond? Did you figure out how to get the wolf, the goat, and the cabbages across the river? Were you able to put the five playing cards in order in ten moves?

Well, here's a surprise for you—all the time you were having fun working out puzzles, you were really doing *mathematics!*

You may think that mathematics just means doing arithmetic problems. That's what many people think. But that's wrong. Arithmetic is really only a very small part of mathematics.

Mathematics is a way of thinking things out, step by step, as you have to do to solve a

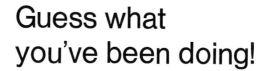

The wolf, the goat, and the cabbages
First, the man took the goat across the river. Then he went back and took the big basket of cabbages across. But when he left the cabbages, he put the goat into the boat. Then he took the goat *back* across the river.

When he reached the side where the wolf was, the man put the wolf into the boat and left the goat. Then he took the wolf across and left it with the cabbages. Finally, he went back and brought the goat across again.

See how easy it was? Were you able to figure it out?

puzzle. It's also a way of using numbers and symbols, as you did to discover Ribidip's magic word. And it's a way of thinking about shapes. A Möbius strip is a shape that has only one side. A maze is a shape that has no inside. Why no inside? Because the beginning and the end of the path do not come together to form a closed shape. And only a closed shape has an inside and an outside.

So, mathematics is really a way of solving all kinds of puzzles and tricky problems. And that can be fun! And useful!

Now that you know a little more about what mathematics really is, go on with this book. You'll find more puzzles, more surprises, a lot of things to think about, and a number of things to do. And you'll find that mathematics is a lot more fun than you ever suspected!

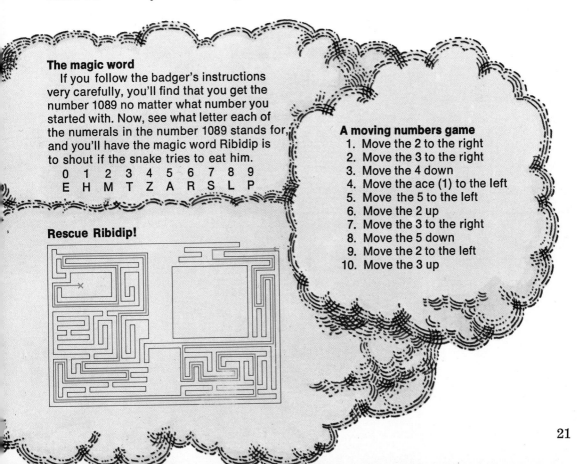

The magic word

If you follow the badger's instructions very carefully, you'll find that you get the number 1089 no matter what number you started with. Now, see what letter each of the numerals in the number 1089 stands for, and you'll have the magic word Ribidip is to shout if the snake tries to eat him.

0	1	2	3	4	5	6	7	8	9
E	H	M	T	Z	A	R	S	L	P

Rescue Ribidip!

A moving numbers game
1. Move the 2 to the right
2. Move the 3 to the right
3. Move the 4 down
4. Move the ace (1) to the left
5. Move the 5 to the left
6. Move the 2 up
7. Move the 3 to the right
8. Move the 5 down
9. Move the 2 to the left
10. Move the 3 up

2

Take a number

Do you know the *color* of number five?
Do you know the *shape* of a four?
Do you know which number is *lucky?*
We can tell you all that and more!

For there's a lore and a magic in numbers,
Or so people thought long ago,
So we'll tell you some things about numbers
That you probably didn't know.

Zero

Zero stands for nothing. If you have zero ice cream cones, then you have none at all.

It may seem very silly to have a numeral for something that isn't there, but the numeral 0 is really very important. The 0 is a placeholder. It shows us how much the other numerals stand for in a number. That's how we know that 10 means ten and 100 means one hundred.

There has always been nothing, but there hasn't always been a zero. The idea of having a numeral that stands for nothing was probably invented in India. The Arabs, who borrowed the idea and brought it to Europe, called the numeral *sifr*, which means "empty."

People in Europe began to use the symbol 0 about a thousand years ago. They changed its name to zero. We still use the Arab word *sifr*, but we spell it cipher (SY fuhr). And for us, *cipher* means zero or any numeral.

One

One is a thing all by itself. But when you put ones together, you get other numbers. You can make every number using ones. You can't do that with any other number.

The ancient Greeks were fond of thinking about numbers and playing with numbers. They often thought of numbers as so many dots, and spent a lot of time arranging dots in different shapes. They thought of one as both a triangle and a square. They also felt that one was the only *real* number, because all other numbers were made from it.

To the Greeks, one was so important they made it their symbol for thinking. We seem to feel that one is important, too. When we say that someone or something is "number one," we mean that it's the very best.

The color of one is said to be red. And in astrology, the number one belongs to the sign of Aries, the Ram.

Two

Two is the first even number—a number that can be broken apart and made into two smaller numbers that are exactly the same. Break two apart and you get a one and a one.

Long ago, both the Chinese and the Greeks thought of even numbers—two, four, six, and so on—as "girl" numbers. The odd numbers were "boy" numbers.

The ancient Greeks felt that the number two was like someone who couldn't make up his mind about something. We still think of two this way. When people say they are "of two minds" about something, they mean they can't decide between two choices.

In the folklore of many lands, the number two stands for opposite things—good and evil, life and death, or light and darkness. The color of two is said to be orange. And in astrology, two belongs to the sign of Taurus, the Bull.

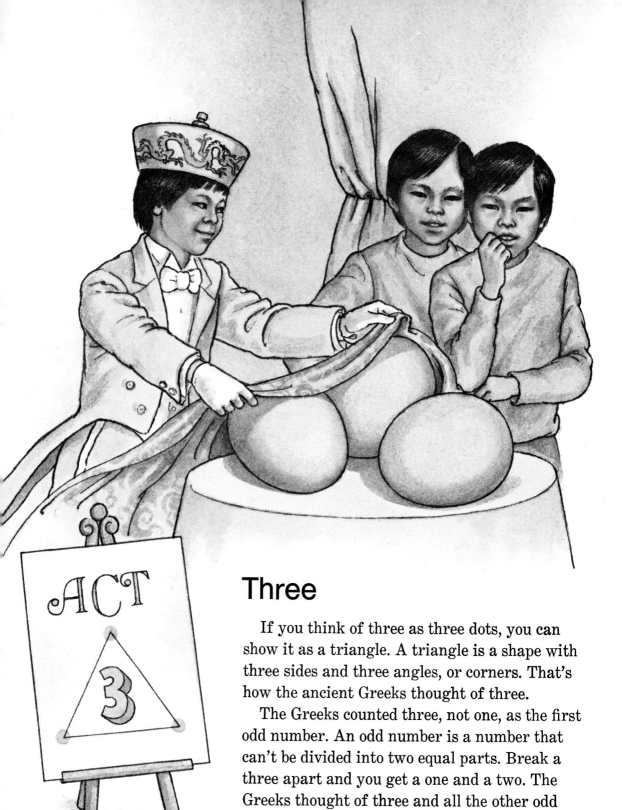

Three

If you think of three as three dots, you can show it as a triangle. A triangle is a shape with three sides and three angles, or corners. That's how the ancient Greeks thought of three.

The Greeks counted three, not one, as the first odd number. An odd number is a number that can't be divided into two equal parts. Break a three apart and you get a one and a two. The Greeks thought of three and all the other odd numbers as "boy" numbers. The even numbers were all "girl" numbers.

For many people of long ago, three was a magical number. It stood for the three parts of life—beginning, middle, and end. It stood for the three "kingdoms" of the earth—animal, vegetable, and mineral. And magicians and witches usually worked in groups of three when casting their magic spells.

The color of three is said to be yellow. And in astrology, the number three belongs to the sign of Gemini, or The Twins.

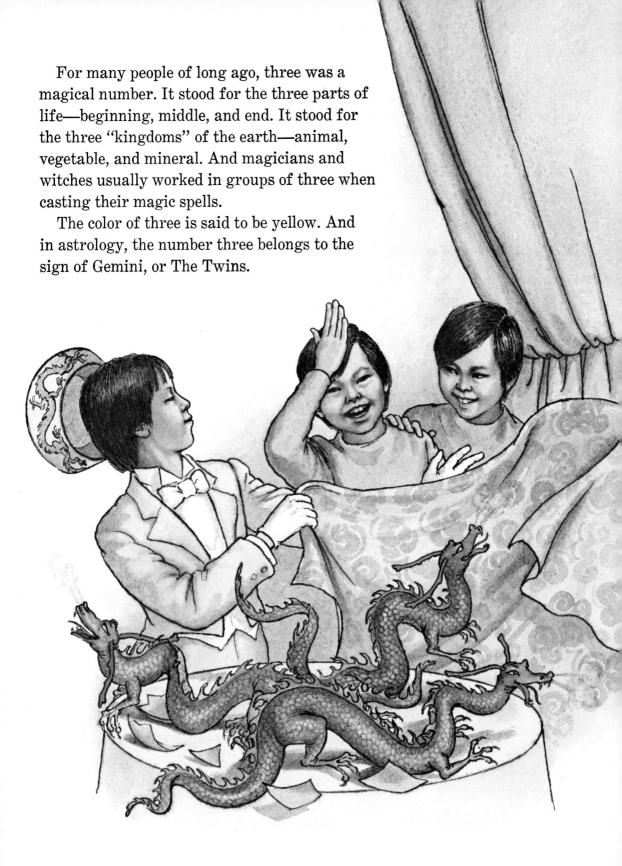

Four

If you think of four as four dots, you can show the dots as a square. And that's how the ancient Greeks thought of four—as a shape with four sides and four corners.

Four is an even number. It can be separated into two equal parts. To the ancient Greeks, justice was a problem that had two equal sides. So the Greeks used four, with its two equal parts, as a symbol for justice.

People of long ago believed that the world was flat, and they spoke of the "four corners" of the earth. And four is the number of the directions, north, south, east, and west.

The color of four is said to be green. And in astrology, four belongs to the sign of Cancer, the Crab.

Five

Think of the number five as five dots that you can arrange in a flat shape that has five sides and five corners, or angles. A shape of this kind is called a pentagon, a name that means "five corners." And that's the way the ancient Greeks thought of five—as having the shape of a pentagon.

To the Greeks, five stood for marriage. For them, five was the first number made of both an odd, or "boy" number, three, and an even, or "girl" number, two. They didn't think of *three* as being made of an odd one and an even two, as we do. For them, one wasn't an odd number.

Five was also thought of as a rather magical number because we have five senses—sight, hearing, smell, touch, and taste.

The color of five is said to be blue. And in astrology, the number five belongs to the sign of Leo, the Lion.

Six

Long ago, the Greeks discovered something very odd about six. It can be divided evenly by three numbers that are less than itself—one, two, and three. And, these three numbers add up to six! Because of this, the Greeks described six as a "perfect" number.

The Greeks thought of six as having two shapes. One shape was a triangle, because six dots can be arranged in the shape of a triangle. And they thought of six as a shape with six sides and six corners. Such a shape is called a hexagon, which means "six corners."

The Greeks thought six was the number that stood for life and for good luck. They also said that six stood for the number of the parts of the human body—two arms, two legs, the head, and the trunk, or body.

The color of six is said to be blue. And in astrology, the number six belongs to the sign of Virgo, the Virgin.

Seven

The ancient Greeks thought of seven as a
shape with seven sides and seven corners. Such
a shape is called a heptagon, which means
"seven corners."

Seven seemed like a special, magical number
to people of long ago—perhaps because they
noticed that the moon changed shape every

seven days. So they did such things as making
a week seven days long and celebrating their
festivals for seven days. Many people still
think of seven as a lucky number.

There are seven colors in a rainbow—violet,
indigo, blue, green, yellow, orange, and red. The
color of seven is said to be violet. And in
astrology, the number seven belongs to the sign
of Libra, the Scales.

Eight

The Greeks of long ago thought of eight as a shape with eight sides and eight corners. Such a shape is called an octagon, a name that means "eight corners." They also saw eight as a shape called a cube, made from two square fours.

The number eight was the Greek symbol for wisdom. And for people of many ancient lands it was the number that stood for magic and science. Ancient Hindus believed that the world was made up of eight parts, and the ancient Chinese divided the year into eight seasons.

The color for eight is said to be rose. And in astrology, eight belongs to the sign of Scorpio, the Scorpion.

Nine

The ancient Greeks thought of nine as a shape with nine sides and nine corners. Such a shape is called a nonagon, which means "nine corners." They also thought of nine as nine dots arranged in the shape of a square.

Nine was a very special number for the people of long ago. You see, they discovered something very strange about it. In any number made up of nines, the numerals add up to nine or are nine. For example, two nines are 18. And the two numerals, 1 and 8, add up to nine. Eleven nines are 99, and each numeral is a nine. And so on. Because of this, nine became a symbol of truth and was said to be a "lucky" number.

All colors belong to nine. And in astrology, nine belongs to the sign of Sagittarius, the Archer.

Ten

The ancient Greeks gave ten a shape with ten sides and ten corners. Such a shape is called a decagon, which means "ten corners." The Greeks also thought of ten as a triangle made out of the first four numbers—1, 2, 3, and 4.

For many ancient people, ten represented a sort of new beginning. In ancient Babylon, the people held a ten-day celebration in honor of springtime, which is a new beginning for all growing things.

In our system of counting, the number ten is a stopping place. After ten, we start over. Our word *eleven* means "ten and one left over." *Twelve* means "ten and two left over." *Thirteen* means "three and ten," and so on. Ten is a stopping place because people learned to count on their fingers—and we have only ten fingers.

In astrology, ten belongs to the sign of Capricorn, the Goat.

3

Fingers, pebbles, and wiggly marks

What would we do without numbers?
Why, we couldn't even count!
We couldn't keep track of birthdays,
Or of any other amount.

But have there *always* been numbers?
Were they always just "lying around"?
Or were numbers a great discovery,
That had to wait to be found?

Counting sheep

How many sheep are there, here?

Two, of course. You didn't have to count them to know that. You could tell at a glance. And you probably don't have to count these sheep either, to know that there are four.

But, without counting, can you tell how many sheep there are in this circle?

You can't? Well, don't be disappointed. Very few people could tell at a glance. In fact, if there are more than five things to look at, all crowded together, people can't tell how many there are without counting.

And that's why counting began. You see, long ago, in prehistoric times, people had no need for counting. They didn't have to be able to count in order to hunt the animals they used for food and clothing. They had no such things as hours, weeks, or months to keep track of. They didn't own much. They had the clothes they wore, and probably a spear and a stone knife. So they didn't need numbers. They simply didn't have anything to count.

But a time finally came when people did need to count. Perhaps it was when they learned to tame animals and keep herds. People who looked after the herds needed some way to make sure no animals had been lost. A person with only three or four sheep could easily keep track of them, of course. But a person with ten or twelve sheep would have just as hard a time telling how many there were as you did in trying to tell how many sheep were in the circle.

So, counting was invented to keep track of large numbers of things.

Fingers for numbers

It was early morning as Amu, the shepherd boy, trudged toward the sheep pen, whistling merrily. His feet were bare. His only clothing was a short skirt made of animal skin. In one hand he carried his lunch, a lump of cheese wrapped in leaves.

When Amu reached the pen, he opened the gate just wide enough for one sheep at a time to come through. As each sheep trotted past him, Amu touched one of his fingers. By the time the last sheep was out, Amu had touched all his fingers but one.

This was how he kept track of his sheep. When he brought them back to the pen, late in the afternoon, he would count them again, on his fingers, to make sure none had been lost.

Amu did not think of his herd as "nine" sheep. He thought of the herd as all his fingers but one. He had no word for "nine," or for any number. He didn't know what a "number" was.

When people first began to keep track of such things as animals in a herd, they simply let their fingers stand for the animals—one finger for each animal. Fingers were the first numbers. And that's how the idea of numbers, and then of counting, began!

Stop at ten

Before people began to count, they probably had no name for any number but one. Suppose a hunter wanted to tell about a small herd of four to six deer he had seen. He might just say it was a "hand" of deer. Then everyone would know that he meant there were about as many deer as there are fingers on a hand. For large numbers of things, people probably just said "many." And "many" might mean anything from ten to one hundred.

But when people first began to count, they

needed a name for every number. There's no way to tell, now, where the names for numbers came from. Perhaps they were made-up words. Or perhaps they were words that meant other things, but were used as "number names."

The people of long ago gave special names to only the first ten numbers. The names for most of the other numbers were just made up using the names of the first ten numbers. The words eleven and twelve sound as if they are special names, but they really aren't. Eleven comes from an Old English word that means "one left over after ten," and twelve means "two left over." Our word thirteen really means "three

and ten." If you say thirteen aloud you'll hear what sounds like "three-ten." The same is true of fourteen through nineteen. And twenty means "two tens," thirty means "three tens," and so on. These number names sound like the number of tens each one stands for.

People gave special names to the first ten numbers because of the way they learned to count. In the beginning, people did all their counting on their fingers. Because they had ten fingers, they counted things by tens. They would count up to ten fingers and then start over. Ten became a sort of "stopping place" in counting. So the first ten numbers were given special names.

People soon decided that the number one hundred was also a stopping place because it was *ten* of something—it was ten tens. So they gave it a special name. Thousand was special, too, because it was also ten of something—ten hundreds. So they gave it a special name.

These "ten numbers" are very important in our system of counting. Think of all the things around you that are broken up into units of ten or are a certain number of tens. A decade is ten years. A century is one hundred years—ten tens. The numbers on a car's speedometer are marked in tens.

But wait a minute, you say, there are lots of things that aren't counted in units of ten. There are twelve inches in a foot. And there are twenty-four hours in a day. There are seven days in a week. And there are twelve months in a year. Why aren't these things in tens? There are reasons, of course. You'll find out what they are when you get to the part of this book called "How long, how fast, how hot, how heavy?"

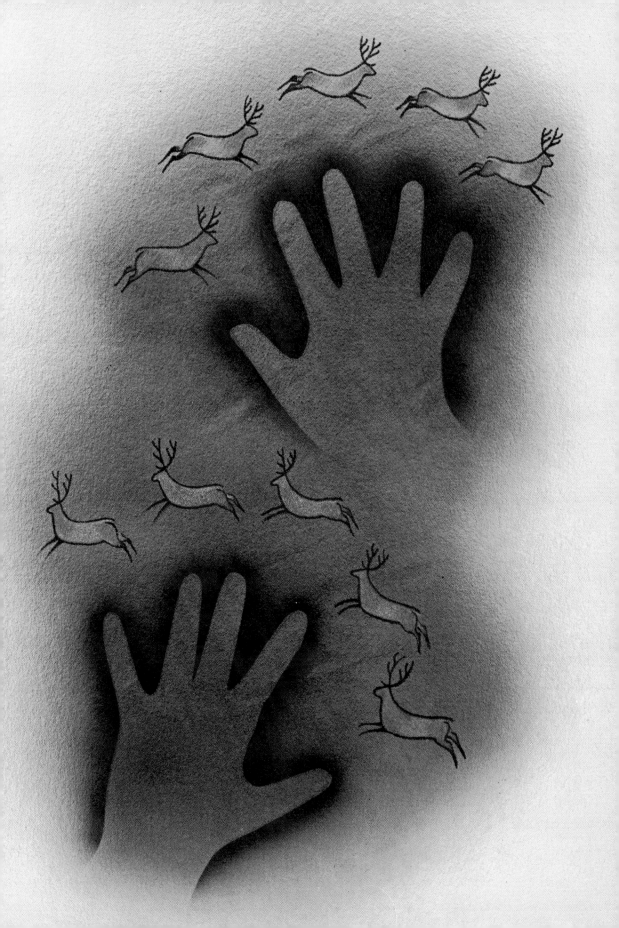

Pebbles for tens

Like everyone else in the family, Mirim had lots of work to do. Even when she was very little, Mirim had helped her mother grind grain for bread and pick berries and grapes. But now that she was seven, she had her first full-time job. Every day it would be her task to watch the family's flock of sheep.

When Mirim's grandfather, Amu, was a little boy, he had watched the sheep. But now there were many more sheep. The flock had grown to nearly fifty. At first, Mirim had trouble keeping count of them.

As she counted each sheep, she touched her fingers. When she had touched all ten fingers, she would say, "There's a ten of sheep." Then she would count another "ten of sheep." But sometimes, she would forget how many tens she had counted, and would have to start over.

However, Mirim was a clever girl. She soon found an answer to her problem. She gathered a number of small pebbles, and each time she counted a "ten of sheep" she put a pebble on the ground. When she had counted the last group of sheep, which came to eight fingers, she looked at the pebbles on the ground. Four pebbles. That meant she had four tens and eight fingers of sheep (forty-eight).

Almost everyone who has ever had to count large numbers of things for the first time must have soon thought of this idea. Using pebbles, notches in sticks, or marks on rocks is a good way to keep a record of the number of things counted. It makes counting any large number of things much easier. And this idea was the beginning of a really marvelous invention—a counting machine.

The marvelous counting machine

Imagine that it is five thousand years ago and that you are a rich merchant in the ancient city of Babylon. You have a curly black beard and a purple robe with yellow fringe at the bottom. You're sitting in a sandy yard, in the shade of a clump of palm trees.

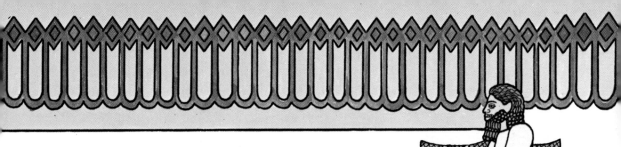

You have a problem you need to solve. In your storehouse there are forty-five baskets of grain. You have just bought forty-three baskets of grain from a farmer. You want to know how many baskets of grain you now have.

With your finger, you draw two grooves in the sand. Next to the grooves you place a small bag full of round, white pebbles. These grooves and pebbles are actually a marvelous counting machine you can use to solve your problem!

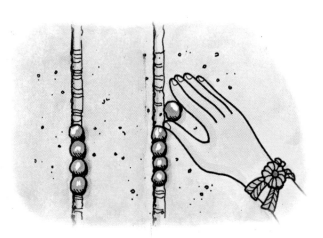

In the right-hand groove you place five of the pebbles. Each of these pebbles has a value of 1, giving you a total of 5. In the left-hand groove, you place four pebbles. Each of the pebbles in this groove has a value of 10, giving you a total of 40. So the pebbles in the two grooves show that you have four tens (40) plus five ones (5), or a total of 45—the number of baskets of grain in your warehouse.

Now you want to add the forty-three baskets of grain you just bought. Taking another handful of pebbles from the bag, you place three pebbles in the ones groove and four pebbles in the tens groove. So you have four tens (40) plus three ones (3), or a total of 43—the number of baskets of grain you just bought.

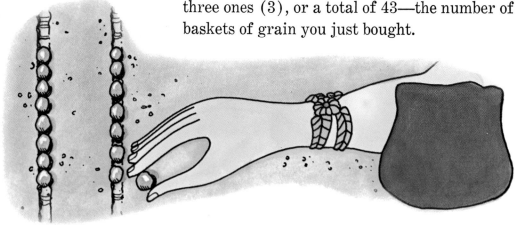

All you have to do now is count the number of pebbles in each groove. In the left-hand, or tens groove, you have eight pebbles, each with a value of 10. Eight tens is 80. In the right-hand, or ones groove, you also have eight pebbles. But each of these pebbles has a value of 1. Eight ones is 8. So you have 80 + 8, or a total of 88. This is how many baskets of grain you have.

If you had needed to, you could have drawn more grooves to work out bigger numbers. If you had drawn a groove to the left of the tens groove, each pebble you put in it would have a value of 100. And if you made another groove to the left of the hundreds groove, each pebble in that groove would have a value of 1,000.

If you think about it, you'll see that we write our numbers today in just the same way they were set up on that ancient counting machine. In a number such as 5,555, the first number on the right stands for five ones (5), the next number to the left stands for five tens (50), the next for five hundreds (500), and the last number on the left stands for five thousand (5,000). In a system of this kind, the value of any numeral depends on where it is placed.

The kind of counting machine an ancient Babylonian merchant used is called an abacus (AB uh kuhs). *Abacus* means "slab" or "table." But this name comes from an ancient word that means "dust" or "sand." The first abacus was probably a tray covered with dust or sand. Counting marks could be made with a finger and erased with a sweep of the hand. After a time, people started making grooves in the sand and using pebbles for counters. Finally, they strung pebbles or beads on wires. They then had a counting machine that was easy to use and could be carried around.

The abacus is a tool that was invented by people in almost every part of the world. The Babylonians and Egyptians used the abacus five thousand years ago. So did the Chinese. And when the Spaniards came to America, they found the Maya Indians using the abacus.

When you buy something in a store, you go up to the counter to pay for it. Have you ever wondered why this table is called a *counter?* It's because, long ago, that's where merchants used their counting board, or abacus. Today, that's where the cash register is. But many shopkeepers in Asia still use an abacus.

An abacus can be used to work all kinds of arithmetic problems. If you know how to use it, you can solve problems very quickly. In fact, there have been contests in which a person using an abacus could do some problems faster than a person using an electronic calculator!

People used to working with an abacus can do arithmetic as quickly as someone using a modern counting machine.

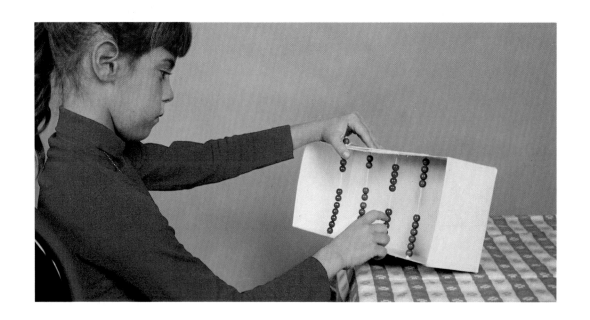

Make your own abacus

An abacus is a lot of fun to use. And you can make one very easily.

To make an abacus like the ones used long ago, you'll need forty pebbles and a piece of cardboard, wood, or stiff paper. With a ruler, draw three lines on the board so that it is divided into four even columns. Then, put ten pebbles, beans, buttons, or pennies in each column and your abacus is ready to use. You'll be able to work with numbers up to 9,999, as shown a little farther on.

For a fancier abacus, you'll need the materials listed below. The best kind of box is a shoebox.

What you will need
a box
string
beads or buttons
scissors
ruler

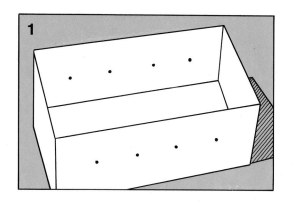

Making an abacus

With the ruler, measure and mark off four equally spaced marks on one side of the box and four marks on the opposite side. The marks must line up. Then punch a small hole in the box at each mark.

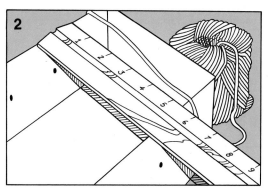

You are going to weave the thread in and out of all the holes, so you will need a piece that is about six times as long as your box is wide. With your ruler, measure the distance across the box, from a top hole to a bottom hole. Cut off a piece of string about six times longer than the distance you measured.

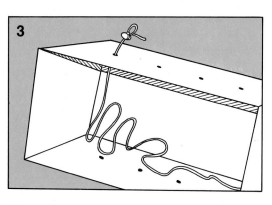

Tie a knot in one end of the string. Slip a bead onto the other end and slide it down to the knot. Push the unknotted end of the string through the first hole on the top left, from the outside to the inside of the box. Pull the string through until the bead is tight against the outside of the box.

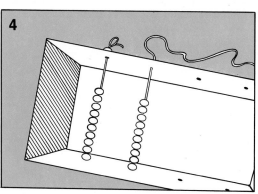

Now slip ten beads onto the string. Push the free end of the string through the opposite hole, from the inside to the outside of the box. Pull the string tight. Then push the free end of the string through the next hole, to the inside of the box. Slip ten more beads onto the string. Push the end of the string through the hole on the opposite side of the box. Pull the string tight.

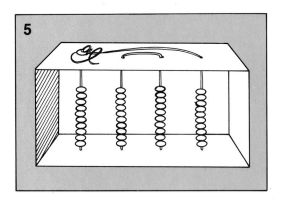

5

Continue threading the string through the holes and putting on beads until you have pushed the end of the string through the last hole on the right. The end of the string will now be on the same side of the box you started from. Pull the string tight and wrap it under the bead holding the other end. Wrap it under the bead several times and tie a knot. With the scissors, snip off any string that's left dangling.

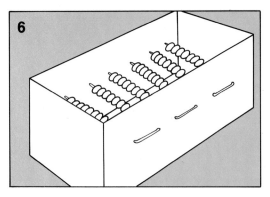

6

You are now ready to work problems with numbers up to 9,999. If you want to work with larger numbers, all you have to do is add more strings of beads. With one more string, you can work with numbers up to 10,000. With two more strings, you can go up to 100,000.

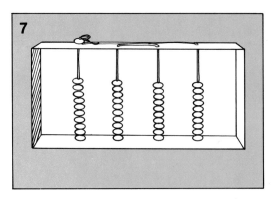

7

How to use an abacus

Working an abacus is easy, but there are a few things to remember. The string on the right is the ones column. Each bead has a value of one (1). The next string is the tens column. Each bead on this string has a value of ten (10). The third string is the hundreds column, and each bead has a value of one hundred (100). The last string, the one on the left, is the thousands column. Each bead on this string has a value of one thousand (1,000).

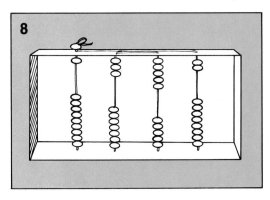

8

You start with all the beads at the bottom, towards you. As you work, you push one or more beads to the top, away from you.

Suppose you want to show the number 1,352. Push up one bead in the thousands column (1,000); push up three beads in the hundreds column (300); push up five beads in the tens column (50); and push up two beads in the ones column (2). You now have 1,000 + 300 + 50 + 2 or 1,352. Now, let's try some problems.

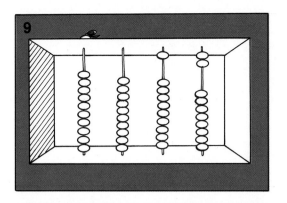

Doing addition on an abacus

Adding on an abacus is quite simple. Start by pushing all the beads to the bottom. Suppose you want to add 12 and 15. The number 12 is the same as 10 and 2. So, push up one bead in the tens column. That's your 10. Then push up two beads in the ones column. That's your 2.

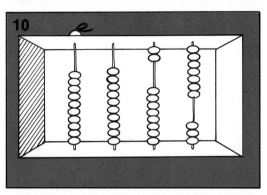

Now, you want to add 15, which is the same as 10 and 5. Push up one bead in the tens column (10) and five beads in the ones column (5).

Now count the beads at the top of each column. There are two beads in the tens column. That's the same as 20. There are seven beads in the ones column. That's the same as 7. And 20 + 7 is 27. And if you write out the problem, you'll see that 15 + 12 is also 27.

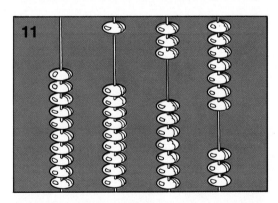

Let's try another addition problem—one that's a little harder. Suppose you want to add 137 and 164. If you write out the problem, you'll see that the answer is 301. But let's prove it on the abacus. Push all the beads to the bottom and you are ready to go.

This time you push up 1 bead in the hundreds column (100), three beads in the tens column (30) and seven beads in the ones column (7). You have 100 + 30 + 7, or 137.

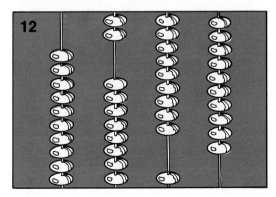

Now, let's add 164 to 137. Push up one bead in the hundreds column (100). Push up six beads in the tens column (60). Finally, push up four beads in the ones column (4).

But wait a minute! You have only three beads left in the ones column. You are one bead short. What happens now?

It's very simple. Push up the three beads in the ones column. You now have ten (10) in the ones column, so you can trade the ten ones for one ten. This is the same as "carrying" in written addition.

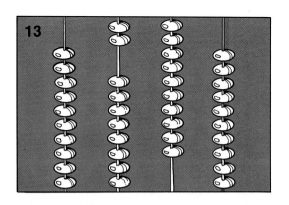

13

To make the trade, move the ten ones to the bottom and move one ten to the top. You now have all your tens at the top and can make another trade.

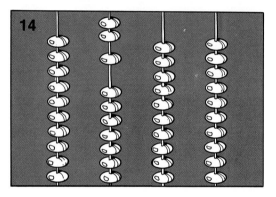

14

Move the ten tens to the bottom and move one of the beads in the hundreds column to the top.

Hold on a minute. You're not through yet. Don't forget the one bead you were short in the ones column that started all the trading.

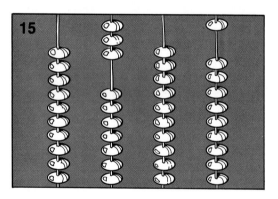

15

You now have plenty of ones, so push one bead in the ones column to the top.

Count your beads and you will see that you have three beads in the hundreds column (300), no beads in the tens column (0), and one bead in the ones column (1), or 301.

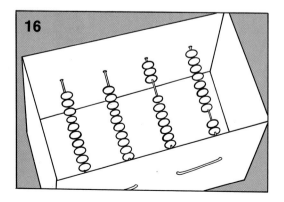

16

Doing subtraction on an abacus

You can subtract, or take away, on your abacus, too. Suppose you want to take 13 from 38 (38—13). Push up three beads in the tens column (30) and eight beads in the ones column (8). You now have 30 and 8, or 38.

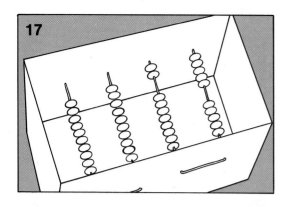

17

You want to take 13 away. Now 13 is the same as 10 and 3. So take away one of the beads in the tens column (10) and three of the beads in the ones column (3).

You now have two tens (20) and five ones (5) left. And 20 and 5 is 25, which is what you get when you subtract 13 from 38.

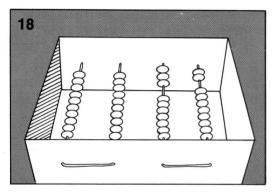

18

Now let's try a subtraction problem in which you have to do some trading.

Suppose you want to take 18 from 32. First, push all the beads to the bottom. Set up the 32 by pushing up three tens (30) and two ones (2).

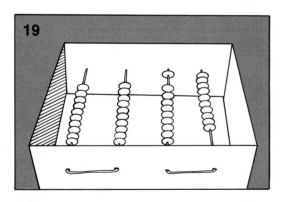

19

You want to take away 18, which is 10 and 8. So push one ten (10) down.

Now you want to push down eight ones (8). But you don't have eight ones at the top, only two. Push the two down. You still need six more. So here is where you must trade. This is the same as "borrowing" in written subtraction. All ten of your ones are now at the bottom, so you can trade them for one ten. Push one ten down and push the ten ones to the top, as shown.

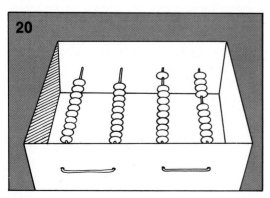

20

You can now push down the six ones you needed. Push them down. Your abacus shows one ten (10) and four ones (4), or 14. And 18 from 32 leaves 14.

And that's how you add and subtract on an abacus.

Now that you know how to use your abacus, try doing some other addition and subtraction problems. You'll be able to use any number up to 9,999. Just remember to be careful when you have to borrow!

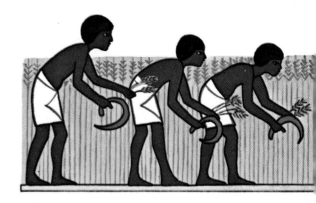

Fingers, flowers, and polliwogs

As tribes became nations and villages became cities, people had more things to keep track of than ever before. Merchants had to keep records of the things they traded to other merchants. The king's tax collectors had to keep a record of the baskets of grain they got.

To do these things, and more, people had to

have a way to write numbers. So, they invented
numerals. Numerals are marks that stand for
numbers. These marks make it possible to keep
written records dealing with numbers.

Some of the first numerals we know of were
invented by the Egyptians about five thousand
years ago. Like people everywhere, Egyptians

counted on their fingers. So, not surprisingly, their written marks for the first nine numerals look like pictures of fingers. They simply used as many pictures of fingers as they needed. For example, six was shown with six fingers.

The Egyptian number system was based on ten. So, for such numbers as ten, one hundred, one thousand, ten thousand, and one hundred thousand, they had special signs.

For the number ten, the Egyptians used an arch, a sort of curve. To write twelve, they used an arch and two fingers. A number such as thirty-three was written with three arches and three fingers. Perhaps the Egyptians picked the curve as their numeral for ten because they thought of it as a kind of enclosure that held the first nine numerals.

The Egyptian numeral for one hundred was a rope with a loop in it. It looks something like a snare used to catch small animals. Perhaps the Egyptians picked this symbol because hunters might set as many as a hundred such traps.

A picture of a lotus flower was the numeral for one thousand. There were thousands of lotus flowers in Egypt's Nile River. So, the Egyptians probably thought a lotus was a good symbol for a big number like a thousand.

The Egyptian number for ten thousand was a bent finger. Perhaps it stood for the finger of the Egyptian ruler, the Pharaoh, who could call ten thousand people together just by beckoning with his finger!

As the numeral for one hundred thousand, the Egyptians used a picture of a tadpole, or polliwog. Millions of frogs lived along the Nile River. When their eggs hatched, the water must have been thick with tadpoles. So it's easy to see why the Egyptians picked the tadpole as the symbol for a number as big as one hundred thousand.

The Egyptians did not have a numeral for zero. Nor did their numerals change in value, as ours do. In our system, 1 all by itself stands for one. But in front of another numeral (as in the number 13), the 1 stands for one ten. The Egyptian mark for one stood *only* for one. It could be placed anywhere in a row of numerals and it still meant one.

The Egyptians usually wrote their numbers from right to left, but they also wrote them from left to right, or even up and down. An Egyptian might have written 1,245 like this:

How would you write 10,582 using ancient Egyptian numerals? All the numerals you need are shown here. Just unscramble them.

Arrowheads, letters, dots

Babylonia was an important kingdom in the
Near East about five thousand years ago. The
Babylonians invented one of the first forms of
writing, and wrote many texts on mathematics.
They did their writing on clay tablets, with a
little stick that made a small mark shaped like
an arrowhead. Their numerals for one to ten
looked like this:

| 1 | 2 | 3 | 4 | 5 | 6 | 7 | 8 | 9 | 10 |

The Greeks of about 2,500 years ago took a different approach. Instead of making up a special sign for each numeral, they simply used the letters of their alphabet. So, their numerals for one to ten looked like this:

A Β Γ Δ E F Z H Θ I
1 2 3 4 5 6 7 8 9 10

The Maya Indians built a great civilization in Central America about 1,800 years ago. They were the only Indians in America to work out an advanced form of writing. And they did a great deal of work with numbers. When they first learned to count, they must have used their fingers *and* their toes, for their number system is based on twenty. Their numerals for one to ten looked like this:

1 2 3 4 5 6 7 8 9 10

About two thousand years ago, the Hindu people of India were using numerals that looked like this:

1 2 3 4 5 6 7 8 9 10

The numerals the Hindus used are of great importance to us. Over many years, and with some changes, they became the numerals we use today!

Fancy fingers

Have you ever seen a clock like the one in the picture below?

The marks on the face of this clock are called Roman numerals. The Romans were people who lived in Italy long ago. We still use their numerals to mark the hours on clocks, for dates on buildings, and other special things.

The Romans seemed to like straight lines, so they made their numerals very straight and stiff. They are also rather fancy, with little crosslines at the top and bottom. But even so, the Roman numerals of 2,500 years ago are really nothing but pictures of fingers. The Roman word for

I  II III IIII V X

finger was *digitus*, from which we get our word *digit* (DIHJ iht). And *digit* means "finger," as well as any numeral from 0 to 9.

As you can see, the numerals for one, two, three, and four are just like fingers held straight up. The numeral for five looks something like an open hand with the fingers held together, away from the thumb. And the numeral for ten looks a bit like two crossed hands.

The early Roman numerals were based on the idea of addition. When the first numeral is larger than the second, the numerals are added.

Much, much later, the idea of subtraction was introduced, mainly to save space. When the first numeral is smaller than the second, it is subtracted from the second numeral. Thus IV means to subtract I from V (1 from 5), or 4.

If you look closely at the picture of the clock face, you will see that it has the early Roman numeral IIII and the later Roman numeral IX. For some reason, clockmakers almost always show these two numerals this way.

For most other numbers, the Romans made combinations of the first ten numerals. Twelve was a ten and two ones, XII. Fifteen was a ten and a five, XV. Twenty was two tens, XX.

Letters were used as symbols for the large numbers. The Romans used L for fifty, C for one hundred, D for five hundred, and M for one thousand.

Can you write 1,528 in Roman numerals?

The numerals now used by Arabic-speaking people are not much like the ones we call Arabic numerals. Only the 1 and the 9 are like ours, as you can see in this multiplication table from a book written in Arabic.

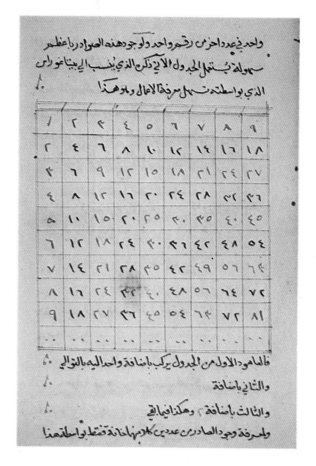

1 A gift from Arabia

The Egyptians used pictures of things for their numerals. The Greeks used the letters of their alphabet for numerals. The Romans used shapes that look like fingers and hands. But where did our numerals come from? Where did we get our wiggly 3 and rounded 8?

The numerals we use were invented by the Hindus in India, about two thousand years ago. We don't know why most of the numerals are shaped the way they are, but we can make a guess about 1, 2, and 3. The numeral 1 very probably stands for one finger, just as in many other number systems. The numeral 2 probably started out as two straight lines that were later connected. And the numeral 3 may have been three straight lines that were later connected. As for the others, well, we just don't know.

The Hindu numerals were adopted by the Arabs. When the Arabs conquered Spain, about 1,300 years ago, they brought these numerals with them. Because the Arabs brought them, they became known as Arabic numerals.

At that time, the people of Europe used Roman numerals. And for several hundred years, they went right on using them. Anyone who had to do arithmetic almost always used an abacus. When you use an abacus, it doesn't matter what kind of number system you use.

But for written arithmetic, the number system can make a big difference. It isn't too difficult to do addition and subtraction with Roman numerals, but they are very clumsy for multiplication and division. This is because they have no place value. On the other hand, in the Arabic number system, the numerals do have place value. And this makes it very easy to work out written problems.

Gradually, European mathematicians began to use Arabic numerals. Still, it wasn't until the first printed books appeared—in which Arabic numerals were used—that most people began to learn these new numerals.

Our numerals didn't always look quite the way they do now, though. Here's how they looked about a thousand years ago:

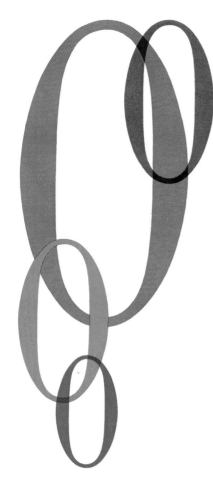

105

The invention of nothing

One of the most important things ever invented was—nothing!

But how can nothing be important? And how can nothing be invented? To understand, we have to go back to the abacus.

To show the number 105 on an abacus, you push up one bead in the hundreds column, no beads in the tens column, and five beads in the ones column.

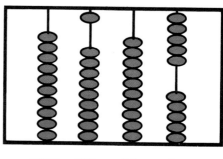

1000's 100's 10's 1's

If you write this number in Egyptian or Roman numerals, here's what it looks like:

In our number system, the order in which the numerals are placed makes a big difference. The numbers 105 and 501 are not the same. That's because the numerals have place value. But in the Egyptian and Roman systems, there was no place value. The numerals could be in any order —the number was the same.

We got our number system from the Arabs, who got it from the Hindus of India. At first, the Hindus had a number system much like other early number systems. They had many numerals —one for each of the first ten numbers, as well as for 20, 60, 80, 100, and so on.

Then, about fifteen hundred years ago, the Hindus did away with all except the first nine numerals. And they invented a new numeral to stand for an *empty* wire on an abacus. They called this numeral *sunya*, or "empty." It was a symbol for *nothing*. With just nine numerals and *sunya*, they could write *any* number!

The Arabs picked up this new symbol and introduced it into Europe. We call the symbol zero, and write it 0. Our word *zero* comes from the Arabic word *sifr*, meaning "empty."

The invention of the numeral 0 to stand for an empty wire on an abacus was very important. In a number system that has place value, the 0 acts as a placeholder. In the number 105, it is the 0 that keeps the 1 in the hundreds place. And this makes it easy for us to do written arithmetic.

Eko, eno, esa

If you speak English, you start by counting, "One, two, three. . . ." If you speak Spanish, you start by counting, "Uno, dos, tres. . . ." And if you speak Ashanti, a language of Africa, you start by counting, "Eko, eno, esa. . . ."

There are special names for the first ten numbers in almost every language. Here are these names in eleven languages. Next to each number-name, you will see how to say it.

		Chinese	Japanese	Hindi (India)	
	write	say	say	write	say
one	一	(ee)	(ee chee)	रूक	(ayk)
two	二	(ur)	(nee)	दो	(doh)
three	三	(san)	(sahn)	तीन	(teen)
four	四	(ssoo)	(shee)	चार	(chahr)
five	五	(woo)	(goh)	पाँच	(pahnch)
six	六	(lyoo)	(roh koo)	हे	(chay)
seven	七	(chee)	(shee chee)	सात	(saht)
eight	八	(bah)	(hah chee)	आठ	(aht)
nine	九	(joo)	(kyoo)	नो	(noh)
ten	十	(shihr)	(joo)	दस	(thuhs)

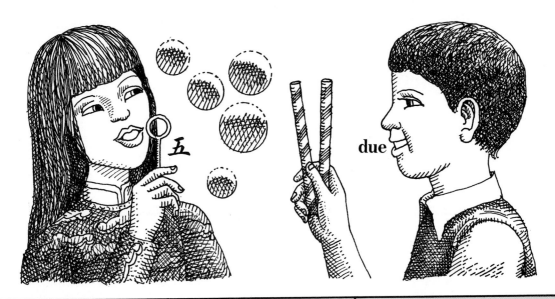

French		Spanish		Italian	
write	**say**	**write**	**say**	**write**	**say**
un	(uhng)	uno	(OO noh)	uno	(OO noh)
deux	(duhr)	dos	(dohs)	due	(DOO ay)
trois	(trwah)	tres	(trehs)	tre	(tray)
quatre	(kah truh)	cuatro	(KWAH troh)	quattro	(KWAHT troh)
cinq	(sangk)	cinco	(THEEN koh or SEEN koh)	cinque	(CHEEN kway)
six	(sees)	seis	(sayz)	sei	(SAY ee)
sept	(seht)	siete	(see EH tay)	sette	(SEHT tay)
huit	(weet)	ocho	(OH choh)	otto	(OHT toh)
neuf	(nuhf)	nueve	(noo EH vay)	nove	(NOH vay)
dix	(dees)	diez	(dee EHTH or dee EHS)	dieci	(DEE ay chee)

nexa

enae

	Cheyenne (American Indian)		Ashanti (Africa)	
	write	say	write	say
one	noka	(NOH kah)	eko	(eh KOH)
two	nexa	(NEKS ah)	eno	(eh NOH)
three	naha	(NAH hah)	esa	(eh SUH)
four	neva	(NEH vah)	enae	(ee NYE)
five	nohona	(NOH hoh nah)	innum	(ih NOOM)
six	naasohtoha	(nah SOH toh hah)	insia	(ihn SEE ah)
seven	nesohtoha	(NEH soh toh hah)	nso	(ehn SOH)
eight	nanotoha	(nah NOH toh hah)	inwotwie	(ihn WAH tweh)
nine	soohtoha	(SOH oh toh hah)	enkoro	(ehn KROH)
ten	mahtohtoha	(mah TOH toh hah)	edu	(eh DOO)

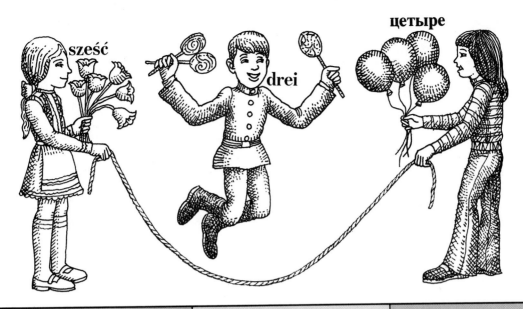

цетыре

szesć

drei

Russian		Polish		German	
write	**say**	**write**	**say**	**write**	**say**
один	(ah DEEN)	jeden	(yeh dehn)	eins	(eyens)
два	(dih VAH)	dwa	(dih VAH)	zwei	(tsveye)
три	(tree)	trzy	(tih SHIH)	drei	(dreye)
цетыре	(cheh TIHR ee)	cztery	(ch TEH ree)	vier	(fihr)
пять	(pih YAHT)	pięć	(pee YENCH)	fünf	(foonhnf)
шесть	(shest)	sześć	(shehshch)	sechs	(sehks)
семь	(syem)	siedem	(SHEH dehm)	sieben	(zee behn)
восемь	(VOH syem)	osiem	(oh SHEHM)	acht	(ahkt)
девять	(DEV yaht)	dziewięc	(jeh VEHNCH)	neun	(noyn)
десять	(DES yaht)	dziesięc	(jeh SHEHNCH)	zehn	(tsehn)

83

What number is this?

10

Counting like a computer

When you see a 1 and 0 together, you would say they stand for ten. But to a computer, they stand for *two!*

We count with ten numerals—0, 1, 2, 3, 4, 5, 6, 7, 8, 9. But a computer uses only two, 1 and 0. So, a computer's numbers don't look like the numbers we are used to seeing. Our eight is 8. But a computer's eight is 1000!

This seems strange, but here's how it works. Our number system has a base of ten. After we reach ten, we start to count by tens. When we reach one hundred (ten tens) we start to count by hundreds, and so on. When we write 235, we're showing that this number is made up of two hundreds, three tens, and five ones:

hundreds	tens	ones
2	3	5

Each numeral is like so many pebbles on an abacus. Its place, or position, shows how much it stands for.

But a computer doesn't use a base of ten. A computer uses a base of two. It doesn't have places for ones, tens, hundreds, and so on. A computer has a ones place, a twos place, a fours place, an eights place, and so on.

When a computer records 2, it does it as 10. This means "one two and no ones." It records 4 as 100. This means "one four, no twos, and no ones":

	four	two	one
2		1	0
4	1	0	0

Here's how the numbers from one to ten look when recorded inside a computer:

Arabic numerals	computer numerals						
	sixty-four	thirty-two	sixteen	eight	four	two	one
1							1
2						1	0
3						1	1
4					1	0	0
5					1	0	1
6					1	1	0
7					1	1	1
8				1	0	0	0
9				1	0	0	1
10				1	0	1	0

For the number one hundred, we write 100. A computer records 1100100. Can you see why?

100	1	1	0	0	1	0	0

What this means is 64 + 32 + 4—which comes to 100. As you can see, a computer simply adds numbers together. But that's a job a computer is really good at. It can add up numbers faster than you can blink an eye!

Counting machines

The abacus was the "great grandparent" of many other kinds of counting machines, such as the adding machine, the cash register, the computer, and the electronic calculator.

It's easy to see where we got the names adding machine and cash register. But why computer and calculator? The name computer comes from a Latin word that means "to count, or reckon." And calculator comes from the Latin word *calculus*, which was what the Romans called a small stone they used for counting. So, you see, it all goes back to counting pebbles, or moving them up and down on an abacus.

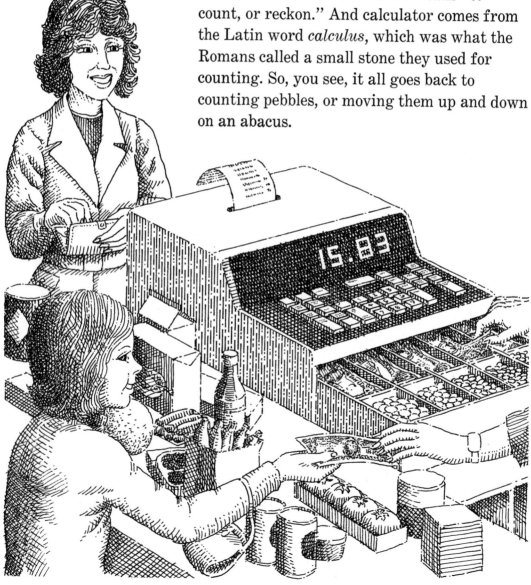

In a grocery store, a machine adds up the prices of the things you've bought. The numbers show how much money you owe.

These children are learning how to use an electronic computer to solve problems.

Many banks and stores use machines to count large numbers of coins.

A pocket calculator is really a kind of modern abacus. You can use it to do arithmetic problems very quickly.

4

What can you do with numbers?

What can you do with numbers?
A lot of surprising things!
You can turn them into pieces and squares,
And into irregular rings.

You can split them into piles,
You can give them funny names,
You can make them into puzzles,
You can put them into games.

You can add onto them forever.
You can make them smaller than small.
In fact, you can do, with a number or two,
Almost anything at all!

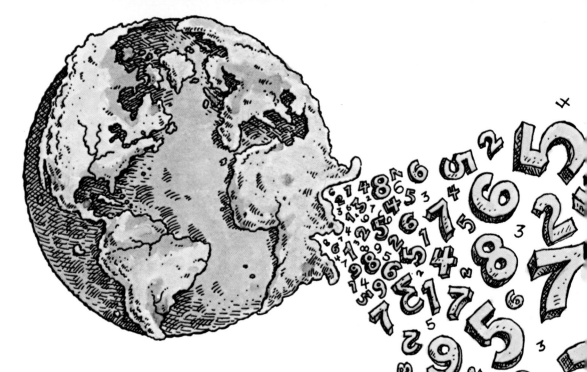

Numbers everywhere

Think of all the numbers you use every day.

At school, you go into a room that probably has a number on the door. Many times during the day, the teacher will tell you the number of a page to turn to in a book. The teacher also gives you a number of pages of homework to do. Perhaps you look at the numbers on the clock, to see if it's nearly time to go home!

At home, you check the clock again, to see if it's time for your favorite TV show. Then you turn to a number on the TV dial to get the channel you want. If you decide to call up a friend, you need to know the right telephone number. Perhaps you'll look at the numbers on a calendar to see how long it is until your birthday, or until a special holiday or event. Before you go to bed, you may step onto a scale and look at the numbers to see how much you weigh.

We use numbers to tell us all sorts of things.

90

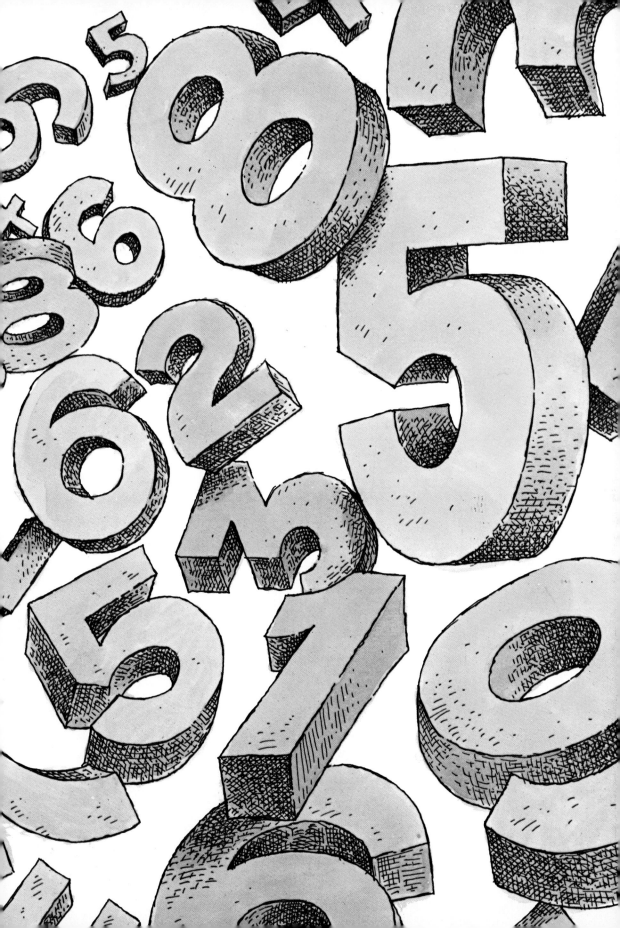

Numbers tell us how hot or cold it is. If your mother takes your temperature, the number the mercury in the thermometer goes to tells your mother if you have a fever.

The numbers on a car's speedometer tell you how fast you are going. And the numbers on roadside signs tell you how fast you may go. Other numbers on signs show how far you are from the place you're going to.

All money stands for numbers. A dollar bill stands for a hundred pennies, or twenty nickels, or ten dimes, or four quarters, or two half-dollars. The numbers on signs in stores show how much things cost.

Think of all the games that are scored with numbers. In football, baseball, basketball, and many other games, the side with the highest number, or score, wins. When you play a game such as Monopoly, or Parcheesi, the numbers you get by spinning a spinner or rolling dice show you the number of spaces you may move.

Numbers are shown with numerals. And with only ten numerals, we can make hundreds of millions of different numbers. There may be millions of people in the city where you live, but they all have different telephone numbers. The street you live on may be many miles long, but no other house on that street has numerals that are arranged in exactly the same way as the numerals on your house—your address. There are many millions of people with cars in the state where you live, but no one else has the same license plate number as the one on your family's car.

As you become older, you will learn of more and more ways in which numbers are used. Airplanes, automobiles, submarines, and many

other things could not be made or used without numbers. Numbers play a big part in the construction of houses and buildings. Numbers help scientists make wonderful new discoveries about all kinds of things. In fact, numbers are so important that we've built giant computers that do nothing but work with numbers to help us solve, in hours, problems that would otherwise take weeks or even years!

You can probably think of many, many other ways we use numbers. It's truly a world full of numbers. In fact, it would be almost impossible for us to get along without numbers!

Milo in Digitopolis

from *The Phantom Tollbooth*
by Norton Juster

The book *The Phantom Tollbooth* is about a boy named Milo and his fantastic adventures in the "Lands Beyond." This is a strange place, where words, names, and expressions mean *exactly* what they say. For example, Milo meets a dog named Tock, who is a watchdog—part watch and part dog! As we pick up the story, Milo, Tock, and a large insect called the Humbug, are driving along a road to the Kingdom of Digitopolis, which is ruled by a person known as the Mathemagician.

"I hope we reach Digitopolis soon," said Milo. "I wonder how far it is."

Up ahead, the road divided into three and, as if in reply to Milo's question, an enormous road sign, pointing in all three directions, stated clearly:

DIGITOPOLIS

5 Miles

1,600 Rods

8,800 Yards

26,400 Feet

316,800 Inches

633,600 Half Inches

AND THEN SOME

"Let's travel by miles," advised the Humbug; "it's shorter."

"Let's travel by half inches," suggested Milo;
"it's quicker."

"But which road should we take?" asked
Tock. "It must make a difference."

As they argued, a most peculiar little figure
stepped nimbly from behind the sign and
approached them, talking all the while, "Yes,
indeed; indeed it does; certainly; my, yes; it
does make a difference; undoubtedly."

He was constructed (for that's really the
only way to describe him) of a large assortment
of lines and angles connected together into one
solid many-sided shape—somewhat like a cube
that's had all its corners cut off and then had
all its corners cut off again.

When he reached the car, the figure doffed
his cap and recited in a loud, clear voice:

"My angles are many.
My sides are not few.
I'm the Dodecahedron.
Who are you?"

"What's a Dodecahedron?" inquired Milo, who was barely able to pronounce the strange word.

"See for yourself," he said, turning around slowly.

"A Dodecahedron is a mathematical shape with twelve faces." Just as he said it, eleven other faces appeared, one on each surface, and each one wore a different expression. "I usually use one at a time," he confided, as all but the smiling one disappeared again. "It saves wear and tear."

"Perhaps you can help us decide which road to take," said Milo.

"By all means," he replied happily. "There's nothing to it. If a small car carrying three people at thirty miles an hour for ten minutes along a road five miles long at 11:35 in the morning starts at the same time as three people who have been traveling in a little automobile at twenty miles an hour for fifteen minutes on another road exactly twice as long as one half the distance of the other, while a dog, a bug, and a boy travel an equal distance in the same time or the same distance in an equal time along a third road in mid-October, then which one arrives first and which is the best way to go?"

"Seventeen!" shouted the Humbug, scribbling furiously on a piece of paper.

"Well, I'm not sure, but—" Milo stammered after several minutes of frantic figuring.

"You'll have to do better than that," scolded

the Dodecahedron, "or you'll never know how far you've gone or whether or not you've ever gotten there."

"I'm not very good at problems," admitted Milo.

"What a shame," sighed the Dodecahedron. "They're so very useful. Why, did you know that if a beaver two feet long with a tail a foot and a half long can build a dam twelve feet high and six feet wide in two days, all you would need to build Boulder Dam is a beaver sixty-eight feet long with a fifty-one foot tail?"

"Where would you find a beaver that big?" grumbled the Humbug as his pencil point snapped.

"I'm sure I don't know," he replied, "but if you did, you'd certainly know what to do with him."

"That's absurd," objected Milo, whose head was spinning from all the numbers and questions.

"That may be true," he acknowledged, "but it's completely accurate, and as long as the answer is right, who cares if the question is wrong? If you want sense, you'll have to make it yourself."

"All three roads arrive at the same place at the same time," interrupted Tock, who had patiently been doing the first problem.

"Correct!" shouted the Dodecahedron. "And I'll take you there myself."

He walked to the sign and quickly spun it around three times. As he did, the three roads vanished and a new one suddenly appeared, heading in the direction that the sign now pointed.

"Is every road five miles from Digitopolis?" asked Milo.

"I'm afraid it has to be," the Dodecahedron replied, leaping onto the back of the car. "It's the only sign we've got."

The new road was quite bumpy and full of stones, and each time they hit one, the Dodecahedron bounced into the air and landed on one of his faces, with a sulk or a smile or a laugh or a frown, depending upon which one it was.

"We'll soon be there," he announced happily, after one of his short flights. "Welcome to the land of numbers."

"Is this the place where numbers are made?" asked Milo as the car lurched again, and this time the Dodecahedron sailed off down the mountainside, head over heels and grunt over grimace, until he landed sad side up at what looked like the entrance to a cave.

"They're not made," he replied, as if nothing had happened. "You have to dig for them. Don't you know anything at all about numbers?"

"Well, I don't think they're very important," snapped Milo, too embarrassed to admit the truth.

"NOT IMPORTANT!" roared the Dodecahedron, turning red with fury. "Could you have tea for two without the two—or three blind mice without the three? Would there be four corners of the earth if there weren't a four? And how would you sail the seven seas without a seven?"

"All I meant was—" began Milo, but the Dodecahedron, overcome with emotion and shouting furiously, carried right on.

"If you had high hopes, how would you know how high they were? And did you know that narrow escapes come in all different widths? Would you travel the whole wide world without ever knowing how wide it was? And how could you do anything at long last," he concluded, waving his arms over his head, "without knowing how long the last was? Why, numbers are the most beautiful and valuable things in the world. Just follow me and I'll show you." He turned on his heel and stalked off into the cave.

"Come along, come along," he shouted from the dark hole. "I can't wait for you all day." And in a moment they'd followed him into the mountain.

"Where are we going?" whispered Milo, for it seemed like the kind of place in which you whispered.

"We're here," he replied with a sweeping gesture. "This is the numbers mine."

Milo squinted into the darkness and saw for
the first time that they had entered a vast
cavern lit only by a soft, eerie glow from the
great stalactites which hung ominously from
the ceiling.

Passages and corridors honeycombed
the walls and wound their way from floor
to ceiling, up and down the sides of the cave.
And, everywhere he looked, Milo saw little
men no bigger than himself busy digging
and chopping, shoveling and scraping, pulling
and tugging carts full of stone from one place
to another.

"Right this way," instructed the
Dodecahedron, "and watch where you step."

"Whose mine is it?" asked Milo, stepping
around two of the loaded wagons.

"BY THE FOUR MILLION EIGHT
HUNDRED AND TWENTY-SEVEN
THOUSAND SIX HUNDRED AND
FIFTY-NINE HAIRS ON MY HEAD,
IT'S MINE, OF COURSE!" bellowed a voice
from across the cavern. And striding toward
them came a figure who could only have been
the Mathemagician.

He was dressed in a long flowing robe
covered entirely with complex mathematical
equations and a tall pointed cap that made him
look very wise. In his left hand he carried a
long staff with a pencil point at one end and a
large rubber eraser at the other.

"It's a lovely mine," apologized the Humbug,
who was always intimidated by loud noises.

"The biggest number mine in the kingdom,"
said the Mathemagician proudly.

"Are there any precious stones in it?" asked
Milo excitedly.

"PRECIOUS STONES!" he roared, even louder than before. And then he leaned over toward Milo and whispered softly, "By the eight million two hundred and forty-seven thousand three hundred and twelve threads in my robe, I'll say there are. Look here."

He reached into one of the carts and pulled out a small object, which he polished vigorously on his robe. When he held it up to the light, it sparkled brightly.

"But that's a five," objected Milo, for that was certainly what it was.

"Exactly," agreed the Mathemagician; "as valuable a jewel as you'll find anywhere. Look at some of the others."

He scooped up a great handful of stones and poured them into Milo's arms. They included all the numbers from one to nine, and even an assortment of zeros.

"We dig them and polish them right here," volunteered the Dodecahedron, pointing to a group of workers busily employed at the buffing wheels; "and then we send them all over the world. Marvelous, aren't they?"

"They are exceptional," said Tock, who had a special fondness for numbers.

"So that's where they come from," said Milo, looking in awe at the glittering collection of numbers. He returned them to the Dodecahedron as carefully as possible but, as he did, one dropped to the floor with a smash and broke in two. The Humbug winced and Milo looked terribly concerned.

"Oh, don't worry about that," said the Mathemagician as he scooped up the pieces. "We use the broken ones for fractions.

"Now," he said, taking a silver whistle from his pocket and blowing it loudly, "let's have some lunch."

Into the cavern rushed eight of the strongest miners carrying an immense caldron which bubbled and sizzled and sent great clouds of savory steam spiraling slowly to the ceiling.

"Perhaps you'd care for something to eat?" said the Mathemagician, offering each of them a heaping bowlful.

"Yes, sir," said Milo, who was beside himself with hunger.

"Thank you," added Tock.

The Humbug made no reply, for he was already too busy eating, and in a moment the three of them had finished absolutely everything they'd been given.

"Please have another portion," said the Mathemagician, filling their bowls once more; and as quickly as they'd finished the first one the second was emptied too.

"Do have some more," suggested the Mathemagician, and they continued to eat just as fast as he filled the plates.

"U-g-g-g-h-h-h," gasped the bug, suddenly realizing that he was twenty-three times hungrier than when he started, "I think I'm starving."

"Me, too," complained Milo, whose stomach felt as empty as he could ever remember; "and I ate so much."

"Yes, it was delicious, wasn't it?" agreed the pleased Dodecahedron, wiping the gravy from several of his mouths. "It's the specialty of the kingdom—subtraction stew."

"I have more of an appetite than when I began," said Tock, leaning weakly against one of the larger rocks.

"Certainly," replied the Mathemagician; "what did you expect? The more you eat, the hungrier you get. Everyone knows that."

"They do?" said Milo doubtfully. "Then how do you ever get enough?"

"Enough?" he said impatiently. "Here in Digitopolis we have our meals when we're full and eat until we're hungry. That way, when you don't have anything at all, you have more than enough. It's a very economical system. You must have been quite stuffed to have eaten so much."

"It's completely logical," explained the Dodecahedron. "The more you want, the less you get, and the less you get, the more you have. Simple arithmetic, that's all."

"Oh dear," said Milo sadly and softly. "I only eat when I'm hungry."

"What a curious idea," said the Mathemagician, raising his staff over his head and scrubbing the rubber end back and forth several times on the ceiling. "The next thing you'll have us believe is that you only sleep when you're tired." And by the time he'd finished the sentence, the cavern, the miners, and the Dodecahedron had vanished, leaving just the four of them standing in the Mathemagician's workshop.

"I often find," he casually explained to his dazed visitors, "that the best way to get from one place to another is to erase everything and begin again. Please make yourself at home."

"Do you always travel that way?" asked Milo as he glanced curiously at the strange circular room, whose sixteen tiny arched windows corresponded exactly to the sixteen points of the compass. Around the entire circumference were numbers from zero to three hundred and sixty, marking the degrees of the circle, and on the floor, walls, tables, chairs, desks, cabinets, and ceiling were labels showing their heights, widths, depths, and distances to and from each other. To one side was a gigantic note pad set on an artist's easel, and from hooks and strings hung a collection of scales, rulers, measures, weights, tapes, and all sorts of other devices for measuring any number of things in every possible way.

"No indeed," replied the Mathemagician,

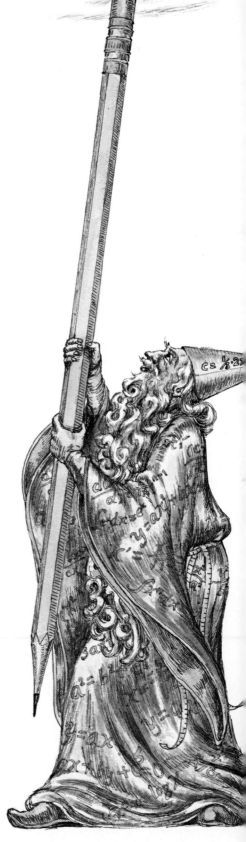

and this time he raised the sharpened end of his staff, drew a thin straight line in the air, and then walked gracefully across it from one side of the room to the other. "Most of the time I take the shortest distance between any two points. And, of course, when I should be in several places at once," he remarked, writing carefully on the note pad, "I simply multiply."

Suddenly there were seven Mathemagicians standing side by side, and each one looked exactly like the other.

"How did you do that?" gasped Milo.

"There's nothing to it," they all said in chorus, "if you have a magic staff." Then six of them canceled themselves out and simply disappeared.

"But it's only a big pencil," the Humbug objected, tapping at it with his cane.

"True enough," agreed the Mathemagician; "but once you learn to use it, there's no end to what you can do."

"Can you make things disappear?" asked Milo.

"Why, certainly," he said, striding over to the easel. "Just step a little closer and watch carefully."

After demonstrating that there was nothing up his sleeves, in his hat, or behind his back, he wrote quickly:

$$4 + 9 - 2 \times 16 + 1 \div 3 \times 6 - 67 + 8 \times 2 \\ - 3 + 26 - 1 \div 34 + 3 \div 7 + 2 - 5 =$$

Then he looked up expectantly.

"Seventeen!" shouted the bug, who always managed to be first with the wrong answer.

"It all comes to zero," corrected Milo.

"Precisely," said the Mathemagician,

making a very theatrical bow, and the entire
line of numbers vanished before their eyes.
"Now is there anything else you'd like to see?"

"Yes, please," said Milo. "Can you show me
the biggest number there is?"

"I'd be delighted," he replied, opening one
of the closet doors. "We keep it right here. It
took four miners just to dig it out."

Inside was the biggest

Milo had ever seen. It was fully twice as high
as the Mathemagician.

"No, that's not what I mean," objected Milo. "Can you show me the longest number there is?"

"Surely," said the Mathemagician, opening another door. "Here it is. It took three carts to carry it here."

Inside this closet was the longest

imaginable. It was just about as wide as the three was high.

"No, no, no, that's not what I mean either," he said, looking helplessly at Tock.

"I think what you would like to see," said the dog, scratching himself just under half-past four, "is the number of greatest possible magnitude."

"Well, why didn't you say so?" said the Mathemagician, who was busily measuring the edge of a raindrop. "What's the greatest number you can think of?"

"Nine trillion, nine hundred ninety-nine billion, nine hundred ninety-nine million, nine hundred ninety-nine thousand, nine hundred ninety-nine," recited Milo breathlessly.

"Very good," said the Mathemagician. "Now add one to it. Now add one again," he repeated when Milo had added the previous one. "Now add one again. Now add one again. Now add one again, Now add one again. Now add one again. Now add one again. Now add—"

"But when can I stop?" pleaded Milo.

"Never," said the Mathemagician with a little smile, "for the number you want is always at least one more than the number you've got, and it's so large that if you started saying it yesterday you wouldn't finish tomorrow."

"Where could you ever find a number so big?" scoffed the Humbug.

"In the same place they have the smallest number there is," he answered helpfully; "and you know what that is."

"One one-millionth?" asked Milo, trying to think of the smallest fraction possible.

"Almost," said the Mathemagician. "Now divide it in half. Now divide it in half again. Now divide it in half again. Now divide it in half again. Now divide it in half again. Now divide it in half again. Now divide—"

"Oh dear," shouted Milo, holding his hands to his ears, "doesn't that ever stop either?"

"How can it," said the Mathemagician, "when you can always take half of whatever you have left until it's so small that if you started to say it right now you'd finish even before you began?"

"Where could you keep anything so tiny?" Milo asked, trying very hard to imagine such a thing.

The Mathemagician stopped what he was doing and explained simply, "Why, in a box

that's so small you can't see it—and that's
kept in a drawer that's so small you can't see it,
in a dresser that's so small you can't see it, in a
house that's so small you can't see it, on a
street that's so small you can't see it, in a city
that's so small you can't see it, which is part of
a country that's so small you can't see it, in a
world that's so small you can't see it."

Then he sat down, fanned himself with a
handkerchief, and continued. "Then, of course,
we keep the whole thing in another box that's
so small you can't see it. If you follow me, I'll
show you where to find it."

They walked to one of the small windows
and there, tied to the sill, was one end of a line
that stretched along the ground and into the
distance until completely out of sight.

"Just follow that line forever," said the
Mathemagician, "and when you reach the end,
turn left. There you'll find the land of Infinity,
where the tallest, the shortest, the biggest, the
smallest, and the most and the least of
everything are kept."

"I really don't have that much time," said
Milo anxiously. "Isn't there a quicker way?"

"Well, you might try this flight of stairs," he
suggested, opening another door and pointing
up. "It goes there, too."

Milo bounded across the room and started
up the stairs two at a time. "Wait for me,
please," he shouted to Tock and the Humbug.
"I'll be gone just a few minutes."

You can follow Milo's further adventures in the
"Lands Beyond" in *The Phantom Tollbooth*. Your
public library probably has a copy of the book.

Magic squares

Have you ever seen a magic square? At one time, people gave all kinds of meanings to magic squares. But of course there is nothing really magic about them. They are just a special arrangement of numbers.

To the left is a magic square that someone in China figured out thousands of years ago. When you add up any three numbers across, or down, or diagonally (slantwise), you always get the same answer! Try it and see.

Below is a different kind of magic square. To use this square, pick any number in it—say 5. Cross out, or cover up, *all* the numbers above and below it, and to the right and left of it.

Next, pick any number that is left—let's say 9. Now cover up the numbers above and below, and to the right or left of the 9.

Now you have three numbers left—1, 5, and 9. Add them up and you'll see that they total 15. No matter what number you start with, you'll always end up with three numbers that total 15! Try it a few times and see.

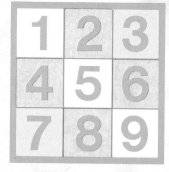

The magic square above is a famous one by the German artist Dürer. It is only a small part of a large picture. But this magic square is more marvelous than most. With all magic squares, you can add up the numbers across, down, or diagonally and the total is the same—in this case 34. But this is only the beginning. Look at some of the other ways you can get 34.

The numbers in the four corners total 34. The four numbers in the center add up to 34. The two middle numbers in the top row, 3 and 2, and the two middle numbers in the bottom row, 15 and 14, total 34. The two numbers in the middle of the first column (5 and 9) and the two in the middle of the last column (8 and 12) add up to 34. And the four numbers in each quarter—such as 16, 3, 5, and 10—total 34!

Why did Dürer pick the number 34 for his magic square? We can't be sure, but there is something very curious about it. He made the engraving when he was 43 years old. This was in the year 1541. Look at the date. Take 1 from 5 and you get 4. Take 1 from 4 and you get 3. So, you get the number 43—the same as his age. Turn 43 around and you get—34!

The magic number in your name

Long ago, many people believed there was a kind of magic in numbers. They thought that numbers could tell about the future and about many other things. So they worked out what they thought were magic ways to use numbers to tell them things.

How would you like to know your "magic number" and what it is supposed to be able to tell you about yourself? Here's how you do it.

Give a number to each letter of the alphabet:

A-1	E-5	I-9	M-4	Q-8	U-3	Y-7
B-2	F-6	J-1	N-5	R-9	V-4	Z-8
C-3	G-7	K-2	O-6	S-1	W-5	
D-4	H-8	L-3	P-7	T-2	X-6	

Then print out your whole name. Don't use a nickname, such as Tom for Thomas, use your real name. Beneath each letter, put the number for that letter, like this:

```
M A R I E   L O U I S E   S M I T H S O N
4 1 9 9 5   3 6 3 9 1 5   1 4 9 2 8 1 6 5
    28    +     27    +       36    =    91
```

Now, add up all the numbers. You'll get an answer with two numerals, such as 91. Add the two numerals together. If you get a number from one to nine, that's your "magic number." If you get a number that's higher than nine, you must then add the two numerals.

For example, Marie Louise Smithson's numbers add up to 91. When she adds 9 and 1, she gets 10. So she adds the 1 and 0 from her 10, and gets 1. That's her "magic number."

When you know your "magic number," look at the list to find out the kind of person you are. Of course, numbers can't *really* tell you about yourself—but it's fun to pretend that there's "number magic."

1. You are sure of yourself, make friends easily, and like to keep busy.

2. You are quiet, rather shy, and work easily with others.

3. You are clever and artistic, and you like being with other people.

4. You are hardworking and dependable. You do not change your mind easily.

5. You are smart, like to be active, and love adventure. But you lose your temper easily.

6. You are fair, unselfish, and careful of other people's feelings. You like to keep things neat and well organized.

7. You like to be by yourself, and you don't like to do what everyone else is doing. You think things out very carefully.

8. You like to plan things out and be sure you are right. You are kindhearted, and people know they can trust you.

9. You like people and you believe strongly in freedom. You are a clear thinker.

Counting squares

Ahmose, chief builder for the king of Egypt, had a problem. He was building a new palace for the king and queen. The floor of the queen's bedroom was to be made of blocks of a special white stone that came from the land of Punt.

Ships would have to go for the blocks and bring them back. So Ahmose had to know exactly how many blocks were needed. If he didn't order enough blocks, the ships would have to go back for more—and the king would be angry. But too many would be a costly waste—and the king would be angry about that, too.

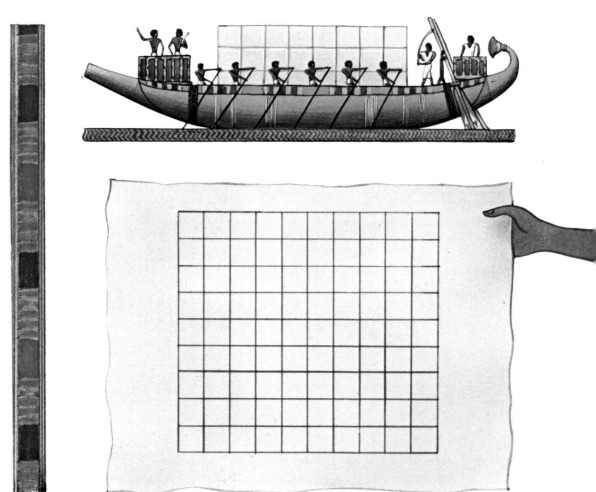

Ahmose began to figure out how many stone blocks he would need. The queen's bedroom was to be ten paces long and nine paces wide. Suppose he had the stone blocks cut into large squares that measured one pace on each side. Then ten of the square blocks in a row would be the exact length of the room. And nine of the squares would be the exact width of the room. Altogether, he would need nine rows, with ten blocks in each row. But how many blocks would that come to?

On a piece of papyrus, Ahmose drew nine rows, with ten squares in each row. He then carefully counted all the squares. There were

ninety squares. That was how many stone blocks he would need.

Of course, you could solve such a problem much more quickly than Ahmose did! All you have to do is multiply the number of blocks in a row (ten) by the number of rows (nine) to get the answer: $9 \times 10 = 90$.

Multiplication is really just a fast way of counting. But for thousands of years, people didn't know about multiplication. When they wanted to know how many bricks were needed for a wall, or how many tiles would cover a floor, they had to draw rows of squares, just as Ahmose did. Then they counted the squares. This worked well enough when only a few tiles or bricks were needed. But if many thousands were needed, the counting took hours.

Then, about five hundred years ago, some bright person got the idea of drawing ten rows of ten squares, and putting a number in each square. Of course, this is what we now call a multiplication table. Five hundred years ago, anyone who did a lot of work with numbers had a copy of this table, just as many people today have pocket calculators. If someone wanted to know what nine times ten was, as Ahmose did, they looked *across* the row that started with nine, and *down* the row that started with ten. And there was the answer!

Today, we learn the multiplication table in school and keep it in our heads. A person of five hundred years ago would be amazed to see how quickly and easily you can multiply, either in your head or using a pencil and paper. Even so, when you do multiplication, you are still really counting squares—just as Ahmose did—only you do it a lot faster!

Multiplication Table

1	2	3	4	5	6	7	8	9	10
2	4	6	8	10	12	14	16	18	20
3	6	9	12	15	18	21	24	27	30
4	8	12	16	20	24	28	32	36	40
5	10	15	20	25	30	35	40	45	50
6	12	18	24	30	36	42	48	54	60
7	14	21	28	35	42	49	56	63	70
8	16	24	32	40	48	56	64	72	80
9	18	27	36	45	54	63	72	81	90
10	20	30	40	50	60	70	80	90	100

Multiplying vampires

Everyone has heard of vampires—those dreadful creatures that live on human blood! According to legend, vampires get blood by coming out at night and biting sleeping people. To stay alive, a vampire has to bite about one person a week. And then, the person who is bitten becomes a vampire, too!

Many people believe there really are such creatures as vampires. But there aren't, of course. And you can use multiplication to prove to your friends that there's no such thing as a vampire.

Here's how you do it. Let's pretend that once there really was a vampire. Suppose this vampire bites one person each week in order to stay alive. And, by the end of the week, the person bitten also becomes a vampire.

The first week, the vampire bites one person. And, by the end of the week, that person is also a vampire. So, at the end of the first week there are two vampires.

1st Week = 2

The second week, each of these vampires bites someone, and both of the people bitten become vampires. So, at the end of the second week, there are four vampires.

2nd Week = 4

The third week, the four vampires bite four more people—so there are now eight vampires!

3rd Week = 8

Do you see what is happening? Each week, the number of vampires is doubling! Doubling is exactly the same thing as multiplying by two. If you double eight, you get sixteen. Or, if you multiply eight by two, you get sixteen. So, by the fourth week, then, there would be sixteen vampires. At the end of the fifth week there would be two times sixteen, or thirty-two vampires, and so on. And, as this keeps on, the number of bloodthirsty vampires grows by leaps and bounds.

4th Week = 16

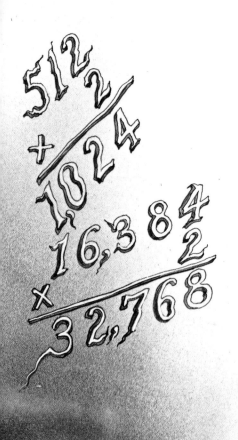

By the tenth week, there would be a total of 1,024 vampires.

By the fifteenth week, there would be 32,768 vampires.

And by the twentieth week, there would be 1,048,536 vampires. That's right—more than a *million* vampires!

By the twenty-fifth week, there would be 33,554,432 vampires. And by the thirtieth week, there would be a total of 1,073,741,824 vampires—more than a *billion* vampires.

And by the thirty-second week, there would be 4,294,967,296 vampires. And that's more than *four billion* vampires.

But wait a minute! There are only about four billion people in the whole world! So you see, if there ever had been just one vampire, every person in the world would have been turned into a vampire in only thirty-two weeks! And because you know very well that you and your friends aren't vampires, you know there never was such a thing as a vampire. See?

$$3 \times 9 = 27 \qquad 27 \times 12345679$$

$$4 \times 9 = 36 \qquad 36 \times 12345679$$

$$5 \times 9 = 45 \qquad 45 \times 12345679$$

Number tricks

Ask a friend if she has a "lucky number." (It can be any number from 1 to 9.) Let's say her lucky number is 6. Tell her that you can show her how to get a whole row of sixes. Here's how:

Have her multiply her lucky number by 9. When she multiplies 6 by 9, she'll get 54. Next, tell her to write the numerals from 1 to 9, but without 8. She should then multiply the number 12345679 by 54. And this is what she'll see:

$$
\begin{array}{r}
12345679 \\
\times 54 \\
\hline
49382716 \\
61728395 \\
\hline
666666666
\end{array}
$$

This trick will work with any number from 1 to 9. Try it and see for yourself.

Here is a puzzle you can have fun with:
On January 1, a girl said to a boy, "Two days ago I was seven, but next year I'll be ten!" She was telling the truth. Try to figure out how this could be possible before you read on.

= 333333333

= 444444444

= 555555555

Here's the way it works: Two days before January 1 would be December 30. On that day, the girl was seven. The next day, December 31, was her birthday. On that day, she was eight. When she spoke to the boy, it was January 1 of a new year. On December 31 of *that* year she would be nine. On December 31 of the *next* year, she would be ten. That's how she could be seven two days ago and ten the next year.

Here's another trick you can use to amaze your friends.

Tell a friend to pick any number, but he is not to tell you what it is. You will tell him!

Have him multiply the number by 2. Then tell him to multiply the answer by 5. Now ask him to tell you that answer. And when he does, you tell him the number he picked!

This is how you do it: Suppose your friend picks the number 25. When he multiplies 25 by 2, he'll get 50. And when he multiplies 50 by 5, he'll get 250. When he tells you the answer, all you have to do is drop the last numeral (in this case, 0) and you have 25—the number your friend started with!

"Girl" numbers
and "boy" numbers

Long ago, when people began to think about numbers, they learned something interesting. When they broke numbers into two parts, two different things happened. Some numbers broke into two *equal* parts. For example, *four* can be broken into two parts that are both *two*.

$$\Big[\Big]\ \Big[\Big]\ \Big[\Big]\ \Big[\Big] = \Big[\Big]\ \Big[\Big] + \Big[\Big]\ \Big[\Big]$$

A number that breaks into two equal parts is called an *even* number.

But when other numbers are broken into two parts, the parts are *unequal*. For example, if you break the number *three* into two parts, you get a *one* and a *two*.

$$\Big[\Big]\ \Big[\Big]\ \Big[\Big] = \Big[\Big] + \Big[\Big]\ \Big[\Big]$$

A number that breaks into two unequal parts is called an *odd* number.

About three thousand years ago, the Chinese called all even numbers, such as 2, 4, 6, and 8,

"girl" numbers. And they called odd numbers, such as 1, 3, 5, 7, and 9, "boy" numbers.

The ancient Greeks decided that 5 stood for marriage, because it was the first number that could be made from a "girl" number, 2, and a "boy" number, 3. (For the Greeks, 1 wasn't a number, so their first odd number was 3.)

With small numbers it's quite easy to tell if a number is odd or even. But how can you tell if a big number, such as 5,284, or 121,336 is odd or even? That's easy, too. Just look at the very last numeral. If it's a 0, 2, 4, 6, or 8, the number is even. And if it's a 1, 3, 5, 7, or 9, the number is odd.

Texas Slim's problem

Texas Slim, the leader of the bandit gang, rubbed his hands together happily. He and his men had just robbed the Pecos bank. They had stolen twenty-one thousand dollars!

"Okay, boys," grinned Slim, "the seven of us will split this up fair and square."

"Hot dawg!" exclaimed Sagebrush Sam. "How much will that be fer each of us, Slim?"

"I don't rightly know," admitted Slim. "I'll just start countin' it out and we'll see. Okay, here's a dollar fer Sagebrush Sam, and one fer Deadeye Pete, and one fer the Sundown Kid, and one fer . . ."

An hour later, while Slim was still counting the money into seven piles, the sheriff and his deputies rode up and captured the whole gang!

When we break a large number into smaller numbers, as Slim was doing, we are dividing it. Slim was dividing twenty-one thousand into seven parts. If he had finished counting all the money into seven piles, there would have been three thousand dollars in each pile.

If poor Slim had gone to school, he'd have known how to do the kind of arithmetic called division. It would have taken him only a few seconds to figure out how much each of his men had coming. Then they wouldn't have been captured. But of course they shouldn't have stolen the money in the first place!

Square numbers

Do you know that there are numbers we call square numbers? Why do we call them *square* numbers? Because they can be shown in the shape of a square!

Remember, every number is made out of *ones*. A number such as four really stands for four *ones*. If you use four pennies (or buttons or dots) to stand for the *ones*, you can arrange the pennies in the shape of a square because four is a square number.

If you look at the squares of pennies shown below, you'll see the first five square numbers. There are two rows of two pennies each in the number four. There are three rows of three pennies each in the number nine. And so on, all the way up to six rows of six pennies each in the square number thirty-six.

Now, how many rows of pennies would it

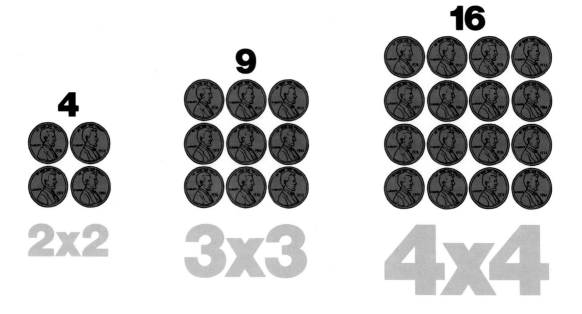

take to make the next square number? That's
right—seven rows of seven pennies each make
forty-nine, the next square number.

To make a square number, you just take any
number and add it together as many times as it
is worth. In other words, if you take the
number six and add it together six times you
get a square number—thirty-six.

When you add numbers together several
times this way, you are multiplying them. And
that's all that multiplication really is—a fast
way of adding a lot of numbers. So, a square
number is simply a number that's made by
multiplying any number by itself—two times
two, three times three, and so on. When you
multiply a number by itself, this is called
"squaring" it.

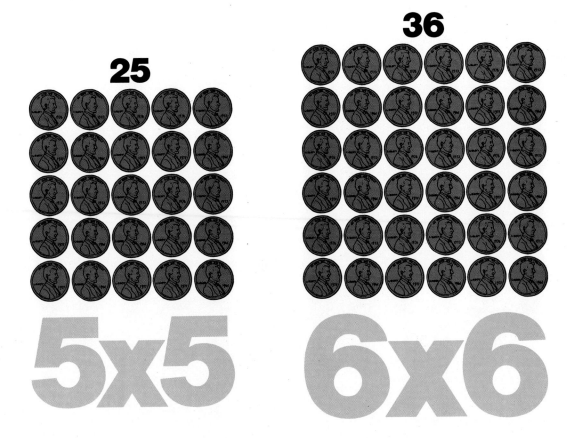

The foolish millionaire and the clever girl

There was once a very rich and greedy man who loved money more than anything else in the world. He knew he had lots of money, but he didn't know exactly how much. So he hired a little girl to count all his money for him.

It took the little girl six days to count all the money. When she finished, she went to the rich man and said, "You have forty-two million dollars."

"Forty-two million!" exclaimed the rich man, and smiled a greedy smile. Then he looked slyly at the little girl. "How much pay do you want for counting the money?" he asked. He thought that because she was only a child, he could trick her into taking a very small amount.

The little girl said, "Well, I worked for six

days, so I think you ought to pay me for six days. Give me two pennies for the first day. Each day after that, just give me the amount you gave me the day before multiplied by itself."

The rich man thought about that. On the first day he would have to give her two pennies. On the second day, he'd have to give her two pennies multiplied by two pennies, or four pennies. On the third day, he'd have to give her four pennies multiplied by four pennies, or sixteen pennies. And on the fourth day, he'd have to give her sixteen pennies multiplied by sixteen pennies, or 256 pennies.

He smiled to himself. Why, at this rate he would only have to give her a few dollars worth of pennies! What a foolish little girl!

So the rich man had his lawyer write up a contract, which both he and the little girl signed. Now, she couldn't change her mind.

On the first day, the rich man paid her two pennies. On the second day, he gave her two pennies times two pennies, or four pennies. Each day after that, he gave her the number of pennies he had given her the day before, multiplied by itself. And by the sixth day, the little girl had *all* the foolish millionaire's money!

Here's what happened:

On the first day the clever girl got two pennies.

On the second day she got two pennies times two pennies, or four pennies.

On the third day she got four pennies times four pennies, or sixteen pennies.

On the fourth day she got sixteen pennies times sixteen pennies, or 256 pennies.

On the fifth day she got 256 pennies times 256 pennies, which is 65,536 pennies.

And on the sixth day she got 65,536 pennies times 65,536 pennies. And that comes to 4,294,967,296 pennies. That's more than four *billion* pennies, which amounts to more than forty-two million dollars! So, the foolish millionaire had to give the clever little girl all his money.

What the foolish millionaire didn't realize
was that he had agreed to *square* the amount of
money the girl received each day. To square a
number, you multiply it by itself. If you then
square the answer, and continue to do this, you
very quickly get a huge number. Most people
don't realize just how quickly this happens.

No one has any trouble squaring a small
number. You know that 2 × 2 is 4. But how
much is 2,000 × 2,000? If you answer quickly,
you might say four thousand (4,000). But it
isn't. It's four million (4,000,000)!

Square the number three and then square
your answer. Then see what happens as you
continue to square each answer!

Building numbers

You have probably put together models of cars and airplanes. You've probably made clay models of animals. But have you ever tried to make a model of a number?

Remember, to get a square number, you multiply any number by itself. If you multiply 2×2, you get the square number 4. A square is a flat shape, so you can make a model of the square number 4 very easily. All you need are four toothpicks and four tiny balls of clay. The four balls of clay stand for the four ones that make up the number four.

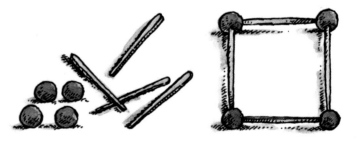

Make two squares like the one shown. Then, join them together with four toothpicks.

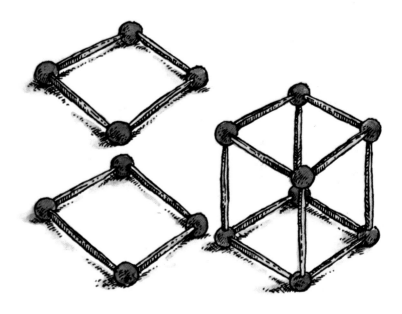

Now, you have a shape called a cube. Count the balls of clay and you'll see there are eight of them. What you've made is a model of the *cubic* number 8.

To make a cubic number, you multiply any number by itself *three* times, such as $2 \times 2 \times 2$. Multiplying the first two numbers gives you a square number—4—and when you multiply by 2 again, you get 8, which is a cubic number. The number 4 is the square of 2, and the number 8 is the cube of 2.

When you cube 3, you multiply $3 \times 3 \times 3$. You get the cubic number 27. Making a model of this cubic number is a real challenge. It would look like this:

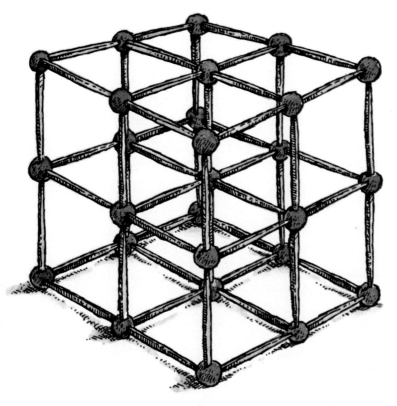

What cubic number do you get when you cube 4 $(4 \times 4 \times 4)$? Try making a model of the number.

The biggest number

What's the very biggest number there is?

Is it a million? That's one followed by six zeros—1,000,000.

No, one million isn't the biggest number. There can be *many* millions. For example, the earth is about 93 million miles (150 million kilometers) from the sun. So there can be numbers that are in the hundreds of millions, the thousands of millions, and even in the millions of millions. The number one million millions is written like this:

1,000,000,000,000

But even a million millions isn't the biggest number. There's a much bigger number that is

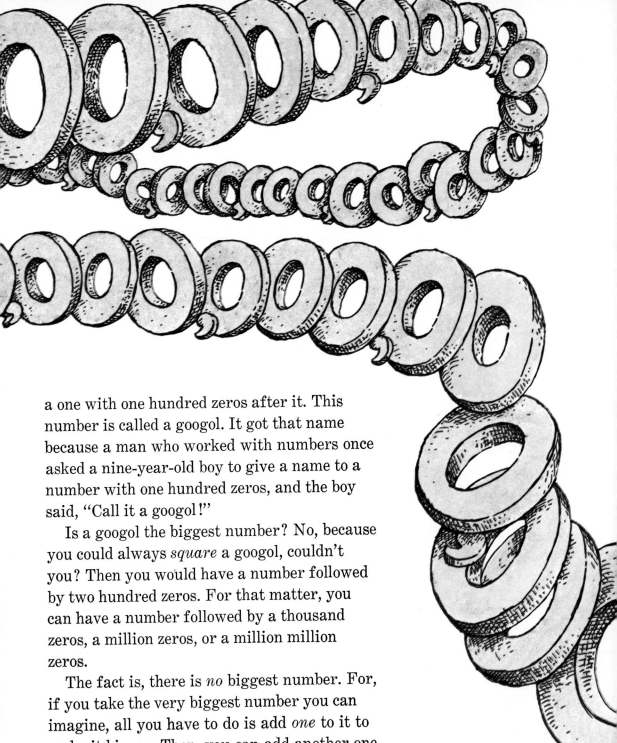

a one with one hundred zeros after it. This
number is called a googol. It got that name
because a man who worked with numbers once
asked a nine-year-old boy to give a name to a
number with one hundred zeros, and the boy
said, "Call it a googol!"

Is a googol the biggest number? No, because
you could always *square* a googol, couldn't
you? Then you would have a number followed
by two hundred zeros. For that matter, you
can have a number followed by a thousand
zeros, a million zeros, or a million million
zeros.

The fact is, there is *no* biggest number. For,
if you take the very biggest number you can
imagine, all you have to do is add *one* to it to
make it bigger. Then, you can add another one
to make it bigger still. And you could go right
on adding ones forever and forever because
numbers are infinite (IHN fuh niht). *Infinite*
means without any end.

The smallest number

There is no biggest number. But is there a *smallest* number?

Well, the number *one* is the smallest of the numbers that we count with. But it isn't really the smallest of *all* numbers.

You see, the number one can be divided, or broken, into smaller numbers called fractions. You can break the number one into two parts, called halves. You can break it into three parts, called thirds. You can break it into fourths, fifths, sixths, sevenths, eighths, ninths, tenths, and so on. You can break it into a hundred parts, called hundredths. You can break it into a thousand-thousandths, and even into as many as a million-millionths!

What is the very smallest number, then? A millionth?

No, because even a millionth can be divided into smaller parts! A millionth can be broken into halves, thirds, tenths, hundredths—and even millionths, too!

Just as there is no biggest number, there is no smallest number either. Every number can be broken into fractions or smaller parts. Every fraction can be broken into smaller fractions. And these smaller fractions can be divided, too. So just as numbers can get bigger forever, they can also get smaller forever.

Bigger is smaller

If someone asked you whether you would rather have three peppermint sticks or four peppermint sticks, you'd answer "four," of course. Four is more than three.

But what if someone asked whether you'd rather have one-fourth of a peppermint stick or one-third? What would you answer to that?

Well, first you would have to know what one-fourth and one-third are. If you broke a peppermint stick into pieces, each piece would be one-part of the whole stick. If you broke the stick into four equal pieces, each piece would be one-fourth. If you broke it into three equal pieces, each would be one-third.

Fourths and thirds—and fifths and sixths and so on—are fractions. Fraction means "broken," and that's what fractions are— broken pieces of a number. We can show fractions with words, such as one-fifth, or with numerals, such as $\frac{1}{5}$. Both mean the same thing.

If you said that you'd rather have one-third ($\frac{1}{3}$) of a peppermint stick than one-fourth ($\frac{1}{4}$), you would be right. When you are counting, four is more than three, but when you're using fractions, one-fourth is *smaller* than one-third.

See for yourself. Here's a peppermint stick that's broken into thirds, and one that's broken into fourths. As you can see, thirds are bigger than fourths.

In fractions, the bigger a number is, the *smaller* the piece is. A sixteenth is much, much smaller than a sixth. And a hundredth is ten times smaller than a tenth!

Tuesday I Was Ten

Tuesday I was ten, and though
The fact delights me plenty,
It sort of startles me to know
I'm now a half of twenty.

It's nice to own a bigger bike
With brakes along the wheels
And figure skates (the kind I like)
And shoes with little heels,
And have a real allowance, too,
To make me wise and thrifty;
But still, I can't believe (can you?)
I'm now a fifth of fifty!

Although an age like ten appears
Quite young and un-adventure-y,
My gosh! In only ninety years
My age will be a century!

Kaye Starbird

Pie puzzles

Fractions are foolers. For this reason, they make good puzzles.

Here's a puzzle about different fractions of apple, cherry, and blueberry pie.

Would you rather have the one piece of apple, the three pieces of cherry, or the two pieces of blueberry pie? You'd get more if you took the one piece of apple? Let's see.

Cut a cherry pie into six equal pieces.

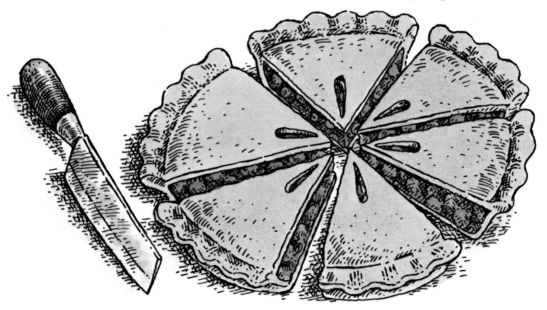

Each piece is one-sixth ($\frac{1}{6}$) of the pie. Take three of the sixths ($\frac{3}{6}$), put them together,

and you have half ($\frac{1}{2}$) a pie. So, the fraction $\frac{3}{6}$ is the same as the fraction $\frac{1}{2}$.

Cut a blueberry pie into four equal pieces.

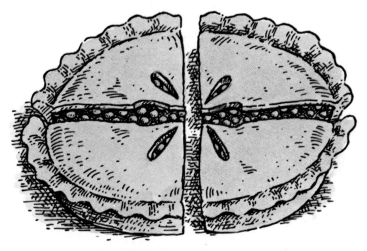

Each piece is one-fourth ($\frac{1}{4}$) of the pie. Take two of the fourths ($\frac{2}{4}$), put them together,

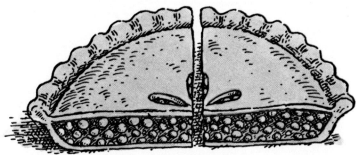

and you have half ($\frac{1}{2}$) a pie. So, the fractions $\frac{2}{4}$, $\frac{3}{6}$, and $\frac{1}{2}$ are all the same amount of pie!

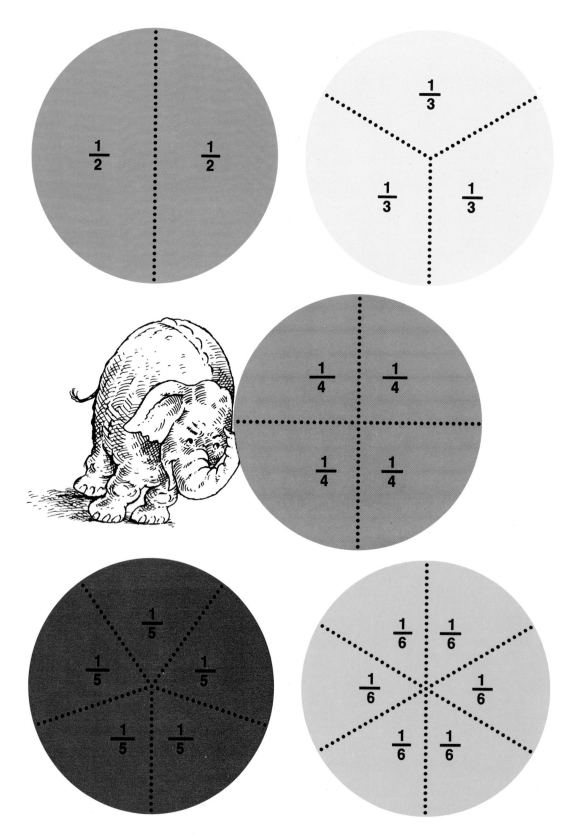

150

Fraction fun

On the opposite page there are five circles. Trace each of these circles on a piece of paper. Be sure to trace all the lines and numbers inside the circles. Then cut out each circle. After you have done this, cut the circles into fractions by cutting along the dotted lines.

Now, mix all the pieces together. Then see how many different ways you can put them together to make circles again!

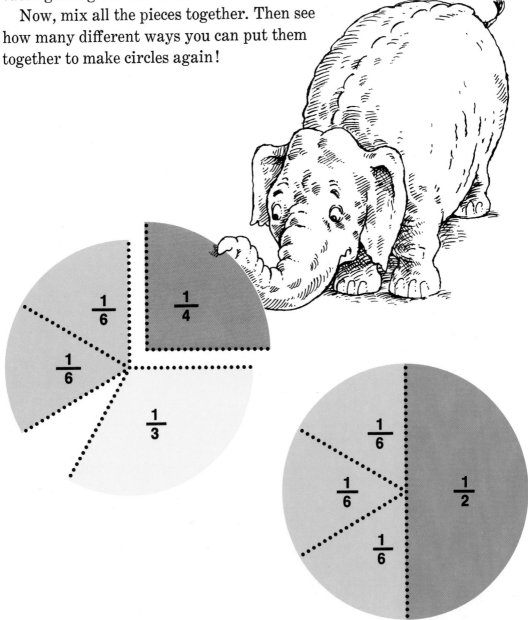

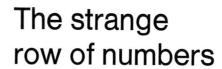

The strange row of numbers

Just for fun, a mathematician once made up a puzzle about rabbits. It went like this.

Suppose that you have a boy rabbit and a girl rabbit. Each month, your pair of rabbits has a boy rabbit and a girl rabbit. Suppose each pair of baby rabbits is grown up in just two months. Then they have a pair of baby rabbits each month. How many rabbits will there be at the end of a year?

You can figure it out quite easily for a while. First, there are two rabbits.

By the end of one month, the two rabbits have a pair of baby rabbits. So now you have four rabbits.

By the end of the second month, the first two rabbits have another pair of babies. Now there are six rabbits altogether.

In the third month, things begin to get harder to figure out. The first pair of rabbits have another pair of babies. That makes eight rabbits. But now the baby rabbits born in the first month are old enough to have their first pair of babies. So, altogether that makes ten rabbits.

It gets even more complicated during the fourth month. The first rabbits have another pair of babies, making twelve rabbits. The second pair of rabbits also has another pair of babies, making fourteen rabbits. And now the pair of rabbits born in the second month are old enough to have a pair of babies. That makes a total of sixteen rabbits in the fourth month.

As you can see, things are now going to get harder and harder to figure out.

Actually, there's a way of finding out the answer without counting up any more pairs of rabbits! It's hidden in the first five numbers we got by counting up all the rabbits.

Write the five numbers—2, 4, 6, 10, 16—on a piece of paper. Can you see the secret?

If you add up any two numbers that are next to one another, the sum is the same as the following number! Add up the first two numbers, 2 and 4, and you get the third number, 6. Add the second and third numbers, 4 and 6, and you get the fourth number, 10.

Rabbitsville
Population
2
4
6
10
16
26
42
68
110
178
288
466
754

And add the third and fourth numbers, 6 and 10, and you get 16, which is the fifth number!

So you see, you can find out the answer to the rabbit problem simply by adding up two numbers at a time. Add the last two numbers in the column—10 and 16—and then put the new number you get at the end of the column. Then add up the last two numbers you now have. Keep doing this until you have thirteen numbers in the column.

The first number—2—is the number of rabbits that you started with. The next twelve numbers—one number for each month of the year—show how many rabbits you had by the end of each month. The last number is the number of rabbits at the end of the year.

A series of numbers of this sort is called a sequence, which means "a group of things that are connected together." The mathematician who worked out the rabbit puzzle discovered a number sequence that goes 0, 1, 1, 2, 3, 5, 8, 13, 21, 34, and so on.

As you can see, any two numbers that are next to each other add up to the next number. Thus 0 and 1 are 1, 1 and 1 are 2, 1 and 2 are 3, and so on. This sequence is called the Fibonacci sequence (fee buh NAH chee SEE kwuhns), after the man who discovered it.

Now, there's something really strange about the Fibonacci sequence. Nature uses it! The bumps upon a pineapple, the scales on a pine cone, the leaves on the stem of a rose bush, and the little bumps in the head of a daisy are all arranged in the Fibonacci sequence!

For example, if you look at a daisy you'll see that all of the little yellow bumps make up winding rows called spirals. Some of the spirals go to the left and some go to the right.

If you count the spirals that go to the left, you'll see there are 21 of them. Count the spirals that go to the right and you'll see there are 34. And the numbers 21 and 34 are next to one another in the Fibonacci sequence!

If you count the spirals on a pineapple, you'll find there are 8 going one way and 13 going another—and 8 and 13 are next to one another in the Fibonacci sequence. Count the spirals on a pine cone and you'll get the numbers 5 and 8, and they, too, are next to one another in the Fibonacci sequence. It looks as if nature uses mathematics, too!

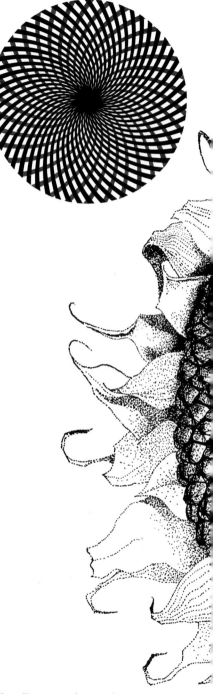

The diagram above shows how the bumps on the head of a giant sunflower form 34 spirals to the left and 55 spirals to the right. The numbers 34 and 55 are next to one another in the Fibonacci sequence.

156

Back and forth and up and down numbers

The number one is more than zero, of course. But can a one ever be *less* than zero?

Yes, it can!

Suppose you are standing at the middle of a long line drawn on the ground. Let's call the place where you're standing zero. Now, if you take two steps forward along the line, you'll be at two *more* than zero, won't you?

But if you take three steps *backward* along the line, you'll be one step farther back than the place you first started from. So, you'll be at one *less* than zero!

You can have many numbers that are less than zero when you're working with what are called positive and negative numbers. The line shown below is called a number scale.

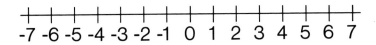

The middle of the number scale is marked zero (0). The numbers to the right of zero are the numbers we count with—one, two, three, and so on. They're called positive numbers. This is because they are *more* than zero. The numbers to the left of zero—the ones that seem to go backward—are called negative numbers. This is because they are *less* than zero.

What good is it to have numbers that are less than zero? Well, negative numbers help us solve a lot of problems with things that go backward and forward and up and down.

Temperature, for example, goes up and down. If you have an outdoor thermometer, you will see that there are numbers above and below zero (0°). The numbers below 0° are negative numbers. So when the temperature is two degrees below zero, we say it is minus two degrees (−2°).

Let's suppose it warms up a little bit and the temperature goes to five degrees above zero (5°). How many degrees has the temperature gone up all together? You can use the number scale to find out. Start at −2 and count up to +5. You'll see that the temperature has gone up seven degrees.

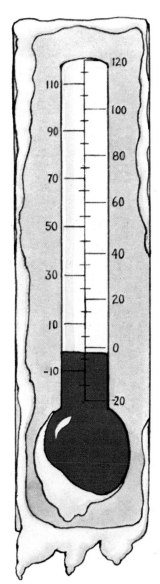

5

What are
your chances?

When you spin a spinner,
Which number is best?
Will one come up
More than all the rest?

When you toss a coin,
Which side do you call?
Is "heads" or "tails"
Most likely to fall?

Is it all just luck?
Is it nothing but chance?
Or is there a way
To tell in advance?

Heads or tails?

Rick wanted to go to the movies and Gayle wanted to go swimming. They decided to toss a coin to see which they would do.

"You call it," said Rick as he flipped the coin.

"Tails never fails!" called Gayle. And sure enough, the coin landed with the tails side up. "See," grinned the girl. "I told you that 'tails never fails!' Swimming it is!"

Do you think that Gayle is right? Do you think that tails will win more often than heads? Or do you think heads is usually the winner?

Try an experiment. Draw a line down the middle of a piece of paper. At the top of the paper, on one side of the line, write "Heads." On the other side, write "Tails." Then, flip a coin fifty times. Each time it comes up heads, make a mark under "Heads" on the paper. If it comes up tails, make a mark under "Tails."

After you've tossed the coin fifty times,
count the marks under "Heads" and "Tails."
You'll find that they're almost even. There
may be a few more heads, or a few more tails,
but chances are there will only be two or three
more of one than the other. And, if you flip
the coin another fifty times, you'll find the
results will be nearly the same.

When you flip a coin, the chance that it will
come up heads is exactly the same as the chance
that it will come up tails. You can't count
on heads coming up more often than tails, or
tails more often than heads.

But suppose you *do* get ten heads in a row,
what then? On the eleventh throw, are you
more likely to get another head or a tail? The
chance that the coin will come up tails is still
exactly the same as the chance that it will come
up heads. Nothing has changed, as you'll find
out if you flip the coin a few more times.

Ali Kwazoor's choice

Prince Ali Kwazoor of Zuristan had been on a long and dangerous journey. He had sailed stormy seas and crossed burning deserts! He had fought fierce dragons and evil monsters! But now, his journey was nearly over. He had reached the Mountain of Darkness. And there, in a cave on the mountainside, was the thing he had journeyed so long and far to find—the great Treasure of Samarkand!

As Prince Ali started into the cave, there was a flash of lightning and a clap of thunder. An old man in a flowing robe suddenly appeared.

"Hold, Prince Ali!" cried the old man. "I am the Wizard of Hind, the guardian of the great treasure! You must face one last test before you can have the Treasure of Samarkand!"

The Wizard held out his hands. In each hand was a box. One box was red, the other yellow.

"In the red box there are four pebbles—one black pebble and three white ones," said the Wizard. "In the yellow box there are seven pebbles—three black ones and four white ones. Without looking, you must take a pebble from one of the boxes. If you pick a black pebble, the treasure is yours. But if you pick a white pebble, you will be turned to stone!"

What would you do if you were Prince Ali? Of course, picking a black pebble would be just pure luck. But which box would give him the best chance to pick a black pebble? Ali thought for a moment. Then he had the answer. Do you know which box he decided to pick from?

In the red box there were four pebbles—one of them black. That gave Ali one chance out of four to pick a black pebble. The yellow box had seven pebbles—three of them black. That gave Ali three chances out of seven. Of course, three chances out of seven, or $\frac{3}{7}$, is more than one chance out of four, or $\frac{1}{4}$. So Ali picked a pebble from the yellow box.

You can see for yourself how $\frac{3}{7}$ gives you more chances than $\frac{1}{4}$ does. Put seven pieces of paper, four white pieces and three colored pieces, in a box or hat. Without peeking, pick one piece of paper from the box and then put it back. Do this fifty times. Keep track of the number of times you pick a colored piece. Now do the same thing with four pieces of paper, three white and one colored. You'll find that you picked a colored piece more times from the box that has seven pieces of paper in it than you did from the box that has four pieces.

But what about Prince Ali? Why, he picked a black pebble of course and went home with the great Treasure of Samarkand!

Game chances

You're playing a game of Monopoly with a friend. You're coming to some of his property that has hotels on it. And he's nearing some of your property that also has hotels. If you roll either a 4 or 5 with the dice, you'll land on his property. If he rolls a 6 or a 7, he'll land on your property.

Which of you is most likely to land on the other's property? Or are both your chances just about the same? There's a way to tell!

When you roll two dice, you can get any one of eleven different numbers—from 2 to 12. You just add the number of dots on the top of each die. And you can get most of the numbers in two, three, or more ways.

Do you think that any number or numbers will come up more often than others when you throw two dice? Absolutely! There are exactly thirty-six possible combinations. But some numbers have a much better chance of coming up than others.

For example, there is only one way to get a 12—with a 6 and a 6. So you have only one chance out of thirty-six ($\frac{1}{36}$) to roll a 12. But there are six ways to get a 7, so you have six chances out of thirty-six ($\frac{6}{36}$) to roll a seven.

Try rolling a pair of dice fifty times. Keep track of the numbers that come up. You'll find that 6, 7, and 8 will probably come up most often; 4, 5, 9, and 10 next most often, and 2, 3, 11, and 12 least often.

So your friend has a slightly better chance of throwing either a 6 or a 7 and landing on your property than you do of throwing a 4 or a 5 and landing on his.

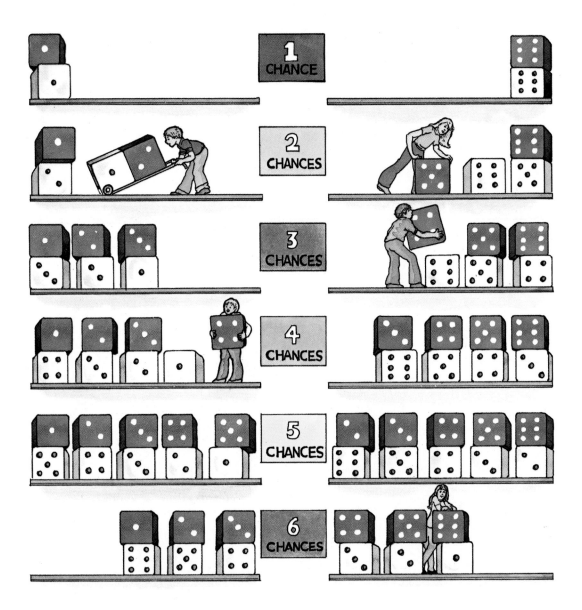

What about games that use only one die? Do you think any one number will come up more often than another when you throw only one die? No, it won't. On one die, there are six numbers, so you have one chance out of six ($\frac{1}{6}$) of getting *any* number. Thus, the chances are even for any number to come up. If you rolled one die a thousand times, you would find that each number would probably come up about the same number of times.

Buttons and boxes

Suppose you have five buttons, each one a different color, and two little boxes. How many ways can you combine the buttons in the two boxes without repeating a combination?

Well, for one, you could put four buttons in one box and one button in the other box. Then you could change that combination four times, just by changing the button that's by itself.

That's five different combinations. But are there any other combinations?

Yes, there are. Do you think you can figure them out? Get yourself five buttons of different colors, or just some scraps of colored paper, and try. You don't really need boxes–just keep the two groups separated. Use crayons and paper to keep a record of each combination. That way, you'll be sure you're not repeating any combination.

Altogether, counting the five combinations already mentioned, there are sixteen different ways to combine the five colored buttons in the two boxes. After you've tried working out the combinations, you can check your results against the pictures at the bottom of the page.

Here are the sixteen possible combinations. To make it easy to check your answers, the buttons are numbered 1, 2, 3, 4, and 5.

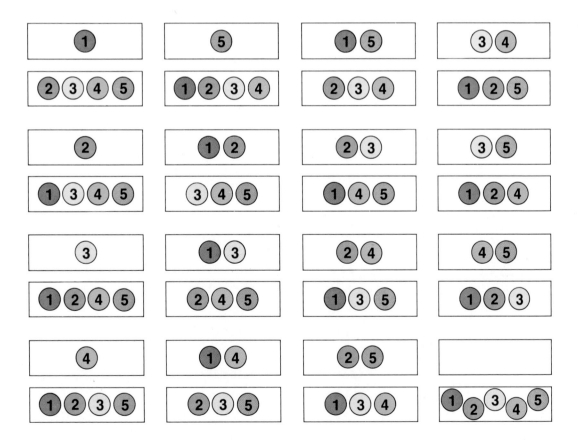

Sharing birthdays

What would you do if you were invited to two birthday parties on the same day?

Well, you would probably go to the party of the person who had asked you first. That would be the fair thing to do. But, you're probably thinking, there's not much chance of being invited to two birthday parties on the same day.

Let's say you have thirty friends. With 365 days in a year, the chance that two friends will have the same birthday is pretty slim, right?

Wrong! The chances are actually better that two people out of any thirty will have the same birthday than that all thirty people will have different birthdays.

There's a simple reason for this. With billions

of people in the world, and only 365 days on which to have birthdays, millions of people share the same birthday. So, in any fairly large group of people, chances are that two or more people will have the same birthday. Among thirty people, the chances are two-to-one that two of them will have the same birthday.

To see how this works, make a "survey" of your family and friends. Find out the birthdays of ten people. Chances are that you won't find anyone with the same birthday. Now, find out the birthdays of ten more people. You *may* find two people who have the same birthday among the twenty people. Finally, find out the birthdays of ten more people. And among all thirty you'll *probably* find two or more people with the same birthday. Try it and see.

Holmes and the *e*

In the story called *Adventure of the Dancing
Men*, Sherlock Holmes, the famous detective,
solves a mystery by figuring out a message that
is in code. Holmes is aware that in English the
letter *e* is used more often than any other
letter. So he decides that the symbol appearing
most often in the code message might stand
for the letter *e*. With that as a start, he is able
to figure out the rest of the message.

But, how did Sherlock Holmes know for
sure that *e* is the most-used letter in English?
How could he have found such a thing out?

Well, here's an experiment for you to try. It will show you what Holmes knew. On a piece of paper, write down the letters of the alphabet. Then, take any page in this book, or any book, and make a record of how many times each letter is used in the first hundred words on the page. Each time a letter is used, make a mark next to that letter on your alphabet list. About nine times out of ten, you'll find that most of your marks are next to *e*.

You can find out all sorts of things in this way. For example, you might make a list of all the sports you can think of—football, baseball, basketball, and so on. Then, ask everyone in your class what their favorite sport is. When they tell you, make a mark next to the name of that sport on your list. When you're through, you'll know which sport is most popular with your classmates.

Records of this sort are called statistics (stuh TIHS tihks). Statistics are very useful in many ways. By means of statistics, governments can find out what sort of crops farmers probably should raise, how many new homes are likely to be needed in coming years, and many, many other things.

6

How long, how fast, how hot, how heavy?

Feet and meters, pounds and grams
Hours and months and days.
How did we come to measure things
In so many different ways?

It all goes back to long ago,
In many ancient lands,
When people began to measure
With fingers, feet, and hands.

They measured time by shadows,
And with dripping water clocks.
They measured years by seasons.
They measured weight with rocks.

So that is how it started,
And oh how far it went!
For now we have a hundred ways
Of doing measurement!

Feet and fingers, hands and arms

On a hillside, near the entrance to a cave, a woman sat busily at work. She wore a dress made of animal skins, and around her neck were strings of beads made of sea shells and animals' teeth. The cave was her home, and the home of her family.

In the woman's lap were some animal skins. The skins had been carefully scraped clean and then dried in the sun. She was sewing the skins together, using a needle that was made of bone and "thread" that was thin strips of leather. When she was finished, the skins would be a jacket for her little boy.

To know how big the jacket should be, she had used her hands to measure the boy and the skins. First, she had found out how many times the length of her hands, held flat, went around the boy's chest and back. Then, after she had

measured the skins the same way, she had cut
them to size with a sharp-edged stone knife.
Soon, her child would have a snug, warm jacket
for the coming winter.

People were probably measuring things long
before they could count. In fact, measuring
may have helped people invent counting. For,
when you measure something, you have to use
numbers to tell its size.

People of long ago didn't have rulers, as we
do. They didn't measure things by inches or
centimeters. Instead, they used parts of the
body for measurement units.

They measured something by seeing how
many hands wide it was, or how many fingers
thick. Another unit of measurement was the
length of the forearm, from the elbow to the
tip of the middle finger. Still another was the
length of the foot, from the heel to the big toe.

We still measure the height of horses in
hands. And we still have a unit of measurement
called a foot.

Balances and coins

When people first began to raise crops, they had to carry the grain from the field to a storage place. They soon learned that they could carry two loads easily by hanging one load at each end of a pole carried across their shoulders. If the loads were about equal, the pole would balance. This gave people the idea for the kind of scale called a balance, for weighing things.

Probably the first thing that people weighed was gold. About six thousand years ago, the ancient Egyptians used weights made of cut and polished stones. Later, they made fancy bronze weights in the form of oxen and ducks.

One reason the Egyptians weighed gold was to keep people from cheating. Only the pharaoh and a few great nobles could own gold. When the pharaoh wanted to have a ring or necklace made, gold was taken from the royal treasury and given to the goldsmiths.

An ancient Greek coin, called a stater, shows the head of Alexander the Great joined with the head of a lion. The name *stater* means "weight."

But there was always a risk. The goldsmiths might try to keep a little of the gold instead of using it all. So, before the gold was given to the goldsmiths, it was always weighed in a balance.

The gold was put into one of the pans of the balance. One or more small weights, shaped like animals, were then put into the other pan until the weights and the gold balanced. And, after the ornament was made, it was weighed—to make sure that the goldsmiths hadn't kept any of the gold.

A Greek drachma, made about 2,300 years ago, shows the god Zeus with an eagle and bears the name of Alexander. *Drachma* means "handful."

After a while, someone came up with the idea of making small pieces of gold or silver that were marked to show their weight. And these weights were the beginning of money—the first coins. That is why some money names were originally the names for units of weight.

The shekel was a unit of weight in Babylonia. It was also the name of an ancient Hebrew silver coin. Today, "shekels" is slang for money. The money unit in Greece is the drachma, and it was originally a unit of weight. The name *drachma* means "handful." In Great Britain, the basic unit of money is the pound. It got this name because at one time it was worth the number of pennies made from a pound of silver.

The Hebrew letters on this silver shekel show that it was made in Judea more than 1,900 years ago. A shekel was also a unit of weight.

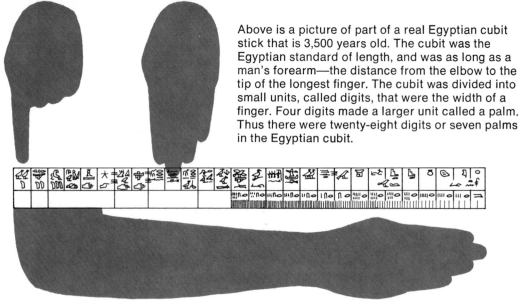

Above is a picture of part of a real Egyptian cubit stick that is 3,500 years old. The cubit was the Egyptian standard of length, and was as long as a man's forearm—the distance from the elbow to the tip of the longest finger. The cubit was divided into small units, called digits, that were the width of a finger. Four digits made a larger unit called a palm. Thus there were twenty-eight digits or seven palms in the Egyptian cubit.

Making things even

There was one trouble with the way people first measured things with their arms, hands, and feet. Some people have longer arms, bigger feet, and wider hands than others. If you and your father each used your feet to measure two boards to be cut five feet long, your father's board would be longer than yours just because his feet are bigger.

People soon realized that a measurement, such as the foot, had to be the same all the time. In other words, they had to have *standard* units of measurement. Then, one person's unit

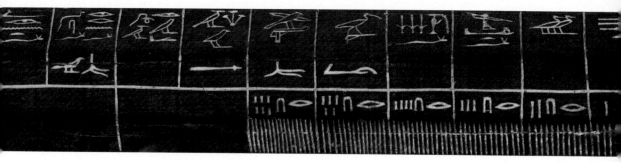

of length, weight, or whatever would be the same as that used by everyone else.

The ancient Egyptians may have been the first people to use standard measurements for length and weight. For example, they had a unit of length called a cubit. To get this length, they measured someone's arm—probably that of the pharaoh—from the elbow to the tip of the middle finger. Then they made a bar of black granite that was exactly this length.

This bar was the official cubit. All other cubit sticks had to be exactly the same length, which was about twenty-one inches (53 centimeters). From then on, if a worker anywhere in Egypt was measuring something in cubits, he would not use his own arm—he would use a cubit stick, just as we use a ruler, a yardstick, or a meter stick.

Nearly six thousand years ago, the Egyptians had a standard unit of weight called a beqa. One beqa weighed about the same as 256 grains of wheat. The actual weights were made of cut and polished stone. The smallest weight found is equal to $\frac{1}{16}$ beqa, or 16 grains of wheat.

Today, all the different units of measurement that we use are based on certain standards. And the stories behind some of these standards are often funny, as you'll see.

Inches, feet, yards, miles

In what is called the English, or customary, system of measurement, there are 12 inches in a foot, 3 feet in a yard, $16\frac{1}{2}$ feet in a rod, and 5,280 feet in a mile. Why such odd numbers? Well, it's because, over the centuries, England was conquered by Romans, Saxons, and other groups of people.

The Romans had a unit called a *pes*, or foot, that was a little shorter than a modern foot. They divided the *pes* into twelve parts. Each part was called an *uncia*, a word that means "a twelfth." As you may have guessed, it's from the word *uncia* that we get the word *inch*. The Romans also had a unit called a *milia passuum*, meaning "a thousand paces." As you may also have guessed, our word *mile* comes from *milia*.

The Saxon invaders had a unit called a *fōt*, or foot, that was a little longer than a modern foot. They divided their *fōt* into twelve equal parts called *thumas*, or thumbs.

These were only a few of the units of length used in England until about seven hundred years ago. Then, King Edward I decided that there should be one standard of length for the entire country.

The king said that three grains of barley would make one inch, twelve inches would make a foot, and that three feet would make an *ulna*, or what we now call a yard. The standard for this new unit of length was an iron bar thirty-six inches long.

Under this law, the new foot was a little longer than the Roman *pes* and a little shorter than the Saxon *fōt*. And this led to a problem. Land was measured in Saxon units. One of these was the rod, equal to 15 Saxon feet. The king didn't dare to change land measurements, so he made the rod equal to $16\frac{1}{2}$ new feet, or the same length as 15 Saxon feet. This meant that the farmers' fields would be the size they had always been.

About four hundred years ago, the queen of England, Elizabeth I, changed the number of feet in the mile. This was done to bring the mile into line with the rod, furlong, and other land measurements. The mile at that time was 4,800 Saxon feet. Well, 4,800 Saxon feet is the *same* distance as 5,280 modern feet. And that's why the mile is now 5,280 feet long.

So we have twelve inches in a foot because the Romans had twelve units in their foot. And we have 5,280 feet in a mile because a king did not dare to change the actual length of a rod.

Pints, quarts, and gallons

People who use the English, or customary, system of measurement buy milk and other liquids in pints (pynts), quarts (kwawrts), and gallons (GAL uhns)—and they have a terrible time remembering that there are two pints in a quart and four quarts, or eight pints, in a gallon. Each of these units is a measure of capacity—the amount of liquid that a bottle or other kind of container can hold.

Today, these liquid measures are based on cubic inches. There are 231 cubic inches in a gallon. In other words, if you had a cube one inch square on the inside, you could pour 231 cubefuls of water into a gallon container. But why are there 231 cubic inches in a gallon? Simply because an English queen had to settle an argument about the tax on wine!

Long ago in England, liquid measure was based on weight, and eight pounds of wine made one gallon. About five hundred years ago, King Henry VII changed the weight of the ounce, which changed the weight of the pound. And, changing the weight of the pound changed the actual weight of a gallon of wine.

The new gallon contained a weight of wheat equal to one hundred of the king's new ounces. The quart contained one-fourth of a gallon. And the pint contained one-eighth of a gallon. The word *quart* comes from a Latin word that means "a fourth." And a quart is a quarter, or one-fourth, of a gallon. The word *gallon* comes from an old word that means "a bowl that holds liquid." And *pint* may come from an old Dutch word that means "plug."

You might think that the new standards would settle matters. But they didn't. People went right on using a number of different "pounds." So, of course, there was more than one "gallon." This meant that a merchant who used a large gallon and one who used a small gallon paid the *same* tax.

Finally, about 270 years ago, the merchants and tax collectors asked the government to solve the problem. After some study, the queen, whose name was Anne, ordered that the "gallon" used most often was to be the standard gallon. It just so happened that this "gallon" contained exactly 231 cubic inches. That's why there are 231 cubic inches in today's gallon!

Ounces and pounds

In the English, or customary, system of measurement, bread, butter, people, and many other things are weighed in ounces and pounds. But why are there sixteen ounces in a pound? And why do ounce and pound have the strange abbreviations oz. and lb.?

Well, it all goes back to the Romans. The Romans had a small unit of weight called an *uncia*. Twelve of these made what they called a *libra*. The English followed the Roman system of twelve small units in one large unit. They called their small unit an ounce, from the Latin word *uncia*, which means "a twelfth." They called their larger unit a pound, from the Latin word *pondus*, which means "a weight."

Uncia, of course, is the same word from which we get inch. But if inch and ounce come from the same word, why are they pronounced and spelled differently? It's really quite simple. Inch came directly from Latin. But ounce came through French. The Old French word was *unce*. So, we say and spell *ounce* much the way the French did.

All weights were once based on the weight of grains of wheat. There were so many grains to

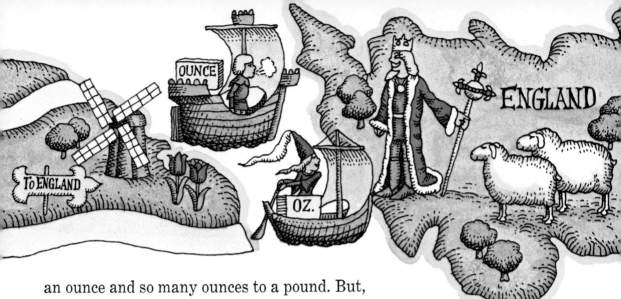

an ounce and so many ounces to a pound. But, for a long, long, time, there were "ounces" of different weights and "pounds" of different weights. Even so, things worked fairly well for hundreds of years. Then, about seven hundred years ago, England began to sell a lot of wool in Europe. As this trade became more important, it led to changes in the system of weights.

Finally, in the year 1340, King Edward III of England set new standards for the ounce and the pound. At that time, most of England's wool trade was with Italy. So, to make trade easier, the new ounce was to weigh the same number of grains as the Italian ounce. At the same time, it was decided that the new pound was to have sixteen ounces. And that's how an ounce became a sixteenth of a pound, even though *ounce* really means "a twelfth."

But why the abbreviations oz. and lb.? They don't seem to have anything to do with the words *ounce* and *pound*. Well, the Italian merchants of King Edward's time called an ounce an *onza*, and used the abbreviation oz. The English merchants just picked up oz. from the Italians. As for lb., it goes back to the Romans. It comes from the Latin word *libra*, their name for a weight of about one pound.

So many measures!

Which weighs more, a pound of feathers or a pound of gold? You probably said, "Ha, you can't fool me! A pound is a pound. They both weigh the same!"

Sorry, you're wrong. A pound of feathers weighs more than a pound of gold!

Of course, it's a trick question. You see, in the English system of measurement, gold and feathers are weighed by *different* kinds of pounds. Most things are weighed by what is called avoirdupois (av uhr duh POYZ) weight. Avoirdupois comes from French words that mean "goods of weight." And there are sixteen ounces in an avoirdupois pound.

Gold, and a few other things, however, are weighed by what is called troy weight. This system of weights gets its name from the

French town of Troyes. And in the troy system there are only twelve ounces in a pound. The sixteen-ounce pound, of course, is heavier than the twelve-ounce one. So a pound of feathers is heavier than a pound of gold.

Here's another trick question for you: Which weighs more, an ounce of gold or an ounce of feathers?

If you said "feathers" this time, then you're wrong! Why? Because an avoirdupois ounce is equal to the weight of 437.5 grains of wheat. But a troy ounce is equal to the weight of 480 grains. So an ounce of gold is heavier than an ounce of feathers.

There are so many weights and measures used around the world that it's impossible for us to remember them all. For example, in the United States, land area is measured in square links, square poles, square chains, and acres. Usually, area is given in acres. The word *acre* means "pasture land." At one time, an acre was as much land as a yoke, or pair, of oxen could plow in one morning.

Have you ever bought a *catty* of tea? You could buy one in parts of Asia. A catty weighs about $1\frac{1}{3}$ pounds (0.6 kilogram). In some places you might still be able to buy a *firkin* of butter. It would last quite a long time, because a firkin is about 56 pounds (25 kilograms).

There are hundreds of special weights and measures. If you keep your eyes open, you may see such units as bolts, butts, carats, cords, ells, fathoms, knots, skeins, and others.

Why are there so many different weights and measures? Why isn't there *one* system we can all use? Well, there is. It's called the metric system. You'll read about it next.

Doing things by tens

About two hundred years ago, there was a big change in the country of France. The French people were being badly mistreated by their king and the nobles. So, the people rose up and got rid of them all. The French then made a new start, with a new government, new laws, and many other changes.

One of the changes was in the system of weights and measures. Measurements in France at that time were in a dreadful mess. For one thing, a foot in the north was not the same length as a foot in the south!

A group of scientists was asked to work out a new system of measurement. Not only was the new system to be better than what the French people were using, it was to be better than any other system then in use anywhere.

In some systems of measurement, the length of a human foot, or a number of grains of barley placed side by side, were used as units of length. But for the new system, the scientists did something more exact. They divided the distance from the North Pole to the equator into ten million parts. One part was made the unit of length and called a meter (MEE tuhr).

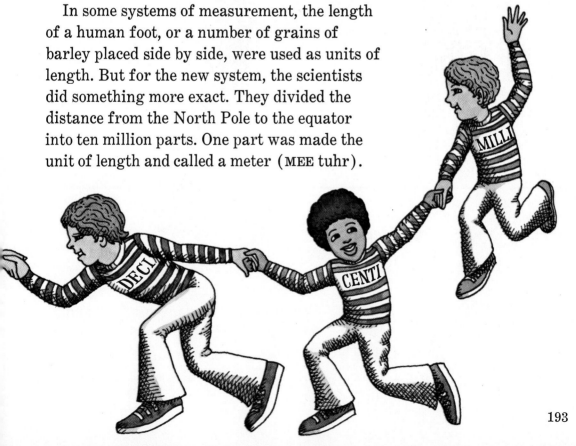

See the Amazing **METRIC MAN**

Grams ⬇ **WEIGHT**

Meters ⬇ **DISTANCE**

Liters ⬇ **CAPACITY**

METRIC MAN

KILO

HECTO

DEKA

CENTI

DECI

MILLI

A meter is slightly longer than a yard, or just a little longer than five *Childcraft* books placed flat, side by side. The word *meter* comes from a Greek word that means "measure." And it is from the word *meter* that the new system, called the metric (MEHT rihk) system, got its name.

The basic units for weight and capacity were worked out using the meter as a standard. The basic unit used to measure weight is the gram (grahm). The name comes from a word that means "small weight." And a gram is a small weight, for it takes 28 grams to equal one ounce.

The basic unit used to measure capacity, or the amount a container will hold, is the liter

(LEE tuhr). The name *liter* comes from an old Greek name for a weight equal to twelve ounces. A liter is slightly more than a quart.

In the English, or customary, system of measurement, there are lots of different names and numbers to remember. But in the metric system there are only a few names. And there is really only *one* number that's used—ten!

All the units in the metric system are based on ten. That is, meters, grams, and liters are all changed to larger or smaller units simply by multiplying or dividing by ten. This change is shown by a prefix. The prefixes are:

For Larger Units

Prefix	Meaning
deka (dehk uh)	10
hecto (hehk tuh)	100
kilo (kihl uh)	1000

For Smaller Units

Prefix	Meaning
deci (dehs uh)	$\frac{1}{10}$ (one-tenth)
centi (sehn tuh)	$\frac{1}{100}$ (one-hundredth)
milli (mihl uh)	$\frac{1}{1000}$ (one-thousandth)

A U.S. penny weighs about 3 grams.

A 12-ounce soda can holds 355 milliliters.

This large paper clip is about 51 millimeters long.

This pencil is about 15 centimeters long.

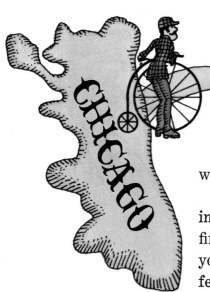

The road distance from Chicago to New York is about 1,290 kilometers.

For example, a *deka*meter is 10 meters long, while a *deci*meter is only $\frac{1}{10}$ meter long.

Do you see how easy it is to work things out in the metric system? In the English system, to find out how many feet there are in 37 miles, you first have to remember that there are 5,280 feet in a mile. Then you have to sit down and multiply 5,280 by 37 to get 195,360—a hard job! But to find out how many meters there are in 37 kilometers is no work at all. The prefix kilo means 1,000, so the word kilometer means 1,000 meters. So, there must be 37,000 meters in 37 kilometers. Easy!

And to make things still easier, only a few of the units of measure in the metric system are ever really used by most people. For example, only four units are generally used to measure length or distance. These are: millimeters, centimeters, meters, and kilometers.

A millimeter (one-thousandth of a meter) is only this long.. It's useful for measuring very small things. Some camera film is measured in millimeters.

A centimeter (one-hundredth of a meter) is this long_____. It is useful for measuring a book or a pencil.

Meters are used to measure everything from the length of a fossil dinosaur skeleton to the height of a mountain. And kilometers, which are one thousand meters long, are used for measuring long distances between cities, or the distance from the Earth to the moon.

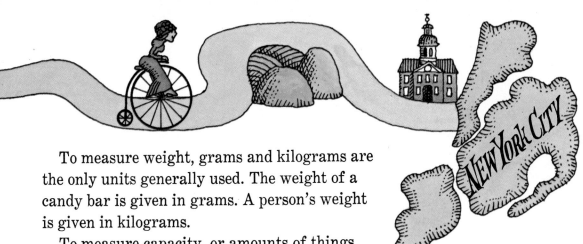

To measure weight, grams and kilograms are the only units generally used. The weight of a candy bar is given in grams. A person's weight is given in kilograms.

To measure capacity, or amounts of things, milliliters and liters are the only units generally used. A tube of toothpaste might hold 100 or 150 milliliters. A carton of milk might hold one, two, or three liters.

Once you become familiar with the metric system it is very easy to use—much easier than the mixed-up English system. The metric system is the best system for measuring things that anyone has worked out yet. It may be the best system that can be worked out.

The average weight of a male Asian elephant is about 4,400 kilograms.

197

Suns and moons, winters and summers

If you want to know what time it is, you look at a watch or a clock. If you want to know the date, you look at a calendar.

A clock measures time during a day. It lets you know when to turn on a favorite television program. A calendar shows time during a year. It tells you how long it will be until your birthday, and on what day it will fall.

Thousands of years ago, people had no need for clocks or calendars. They lived day by day. One day was much like another. Time was not very important. When people had a need to measure time, they did it by "suns," "moons," "winters," or "summers."

A "sun" was one day (twenty-four hours), or the time it took the sun to return to a particular place in the sky. A short journey might take two or three "suns," meaning two or three days.

A "moon" was the length of time from one

full moon to the next. This change in the moon, from round and bright to dark, and then back to round and bright again, takes almost thirty days, or about what we call a month. So, when someone spoke of something that had taken place "many moons ago," they meant many months ago.

When people wanted to speak of something that had happened years before, they would say it had happened "many winters" or "many summers" ago.

It probably wasn't until people learned how to plant crops for their food that they started looking for a better way of measuring time. Then, they had to know when during the year to put seed in the ground. The sun and the moon couldn't tell them when. But the stars could!

Measuring time
by the stars

People of long ago lived out of doors most of the time, so they were used to seeing the stars at night. And they knew that the stars moved across the sky during the year.

Because the stars always followed the same path, and came back to where they started, people learned to recognize the seasons from the stars. When a certain star appeared low in the sky in the spring, they knew that it was time to plow their fields. When the star reached another part of the sky, it was time to plant the seed. Later, the position of another star told them it was time to begin harvesting.

Of course, the stars don't really move. They only seem to move because the Earth moves. The Earth travels around the sun, taking one year to make the complete trip. Thus, a certain group of stars that can be seen in one part of the sky in winter, will be in a different part of the sky in summer.

When people became used to watching for a certain star, they began to think of the time between each appearance of that star as what we call a year. This meant that, depending on which star was used, the year would begin at different times for people of different lands.

The ancient Egyptians started their year in the middle of July, when the star they called Sothis appeared. The Jewish people have always begun the year in the fall. When the Pilgrims came to America, they celebrated New Year's Day on March 25. But today, people in most parts of the world start the year on January 1.

The birth of the calendar

A year is a long time. So, long ago, people decided to divide it into shorter time periods. About five thousand years ago, the Sumerians divided the year into twelve "moons." Each moon had thirty days, so a year had 360 days.

This was the beginning of the calendar. A calendar is just a simple way to keep track of days, weeks, and months. Our word *calendar* goes back to the Roman name for the first day of the month—the day on which bills were due.

Our year, like the Sumerian year, has twelve "moons," or months. But not all the months have thirty days. A good way to remember the number of days in each month is with this poem:

Thirty days hath September,
April, June, and November;
All the rest have thirty-one,
Excepting February alone.
Which hath but twenty-eight, in fine,
Till leap year gives it twenty-nine,

Why do our months have different numbers of days in them? It's so the days will add up to 365. This is the number of days it takes the Earth to go around the sun once. We call this period of time a solar (sun) year.

Actually it takes the Earth just a little longer than 365 days to travel around the sun. In fact,

This Babylonian calendar of about two thousand years ago is made of dried clay. The marks show the days between new moons.

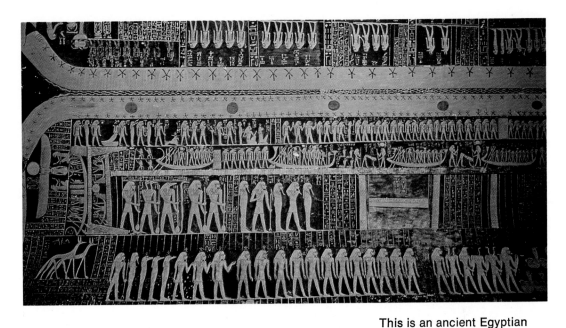

This is an ancient Egyptian calendar found in the tomb of a pharaoh. It shows the months as Egyptian gods.

a solar year has 365 days, 5 hours, 48 minutes, and 46 seconds—which is almost $365\frac{1}{4}$ days. In four years, this quarter of a day adds up to a difference of one day between the solar year and the calendar year.

To keep the calendar year and the solar year the same, we add an extra day to the calendar every fourth year. We call this fourth year "leap year." The extra day is February 29. This happens only in years that can be divided evenly by four—such as 1980. A calendar for a leap year has twenty-nine days in February.

There is also a shorter time period we call a week. *Week* comes from an Old English word that means "a turning." Long ago, a "week" was the number of days between market days. This might be anything from four to ten days.

Today, a week has seven days. Why seven days? We're not sure. But it may be because ancient people used the moon to keep track of time. And the moon changes its shape in about seven days.

These are two pages from a calendar French sailors used more than three hundred years ago. The days of the month are shown in red.

203

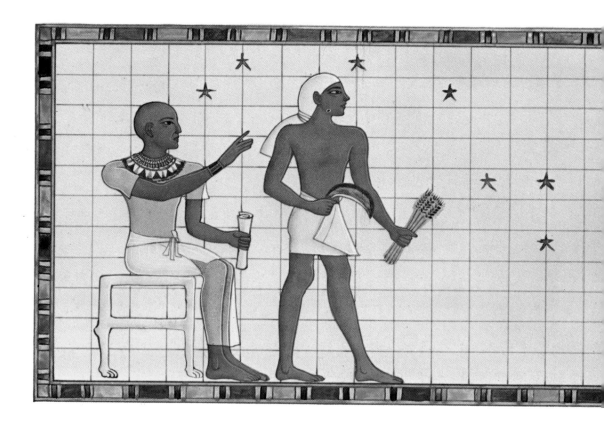

Twenty-four hours a day

Why do we have twenty-four hours in a day? Why not twenty hours? Or sixteen hours?

As a matter of fact, we have twenty-four hours in a day simply because the Egyptians did. They invented the twenty-four hour day long ago, and people have used it ever since!

And why did the ancient Egyptians select twenty-four hours for their day? Actually, they didn't think of it as twenty-four hours, they thought of it as two twelves—twelve hours of daytime and twelve hours of nighttime. And why twelve? Well, they divided the day into ten hours, and then assigned one more hour for the dawn, and one for the dusk, making twelve all together. They gave the same number of hours to the night, to make it even.

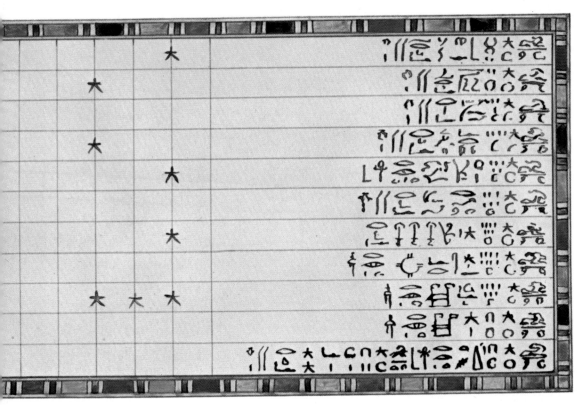

The ancient Egyptians made star charts, such as this, so that they could tell time at night. As each star shown on the chart rose in the sky, a new hour began.

Of course, the Egyptians, whose language was different from ours, didn't use the word *hours*. They used a word that may have sounded something like "wihn oo wiht."

"Wihn oo wiht" meant "priest's duties," and telling time was one of the many duties of the Egyptian priests. The priests marked off the hours during the day by means of clocks that measured the shadow cast by the sun. And they marked off the hours during the night by watching for certain stars to rise on the eastern horizon. As each of these stars appeared, a new hour, or "wihn oo wiht" began.

The ancient Egyptians, and also the Romans, began and ended their day at midnight, as most people do now. The Babylonians and the Greeks began their day at sunrise. And the ancient Jews began their day at sunset.

205

Sun clocks

A clock certainly seems nothing like a ruler. Yet, a clock and a ruler do the same kind of job. They both measure something. A ruler measures length and a clock measures time.

People of long ago used the sun as a clock. They awoke when the sun came up and went to bed when it set. During the day, they were able to judge how much daylight was left by where the sun was in the sky.

By about six thousand years ago, people had learned to use shadows as a way of measuring time. Of course, shadows depend entirely on the sun. The shadow of a tree is very long early in the morning, but grows shorter as the sun rises higher. At midday, with the sun almost overhead, the shadow may nearly disappear. Then, in the afternoon, the shadow begins to grow longer again, but in a different direction.

People soon realized that by pushing a stick into the ground, they could make a shadow. Putting stones or marks along the path of the shadow, they divided a day into periods of

The ancient Egyptians used a T-shaped sun clock to tell time. The shadow of the T, moving along the bar, showed the hour.

The Greeks and Romans of about three thousand years ago told time by sun clocks such as this one. The lines inside the curve stand for hours. The shadow of the pointer, moving across the lines, showed the time.

time. Thus, one person could say to another, "Let's meet tomorrow morning, when the shadow touches the second mark."

More than three thousand years ago, the priests of ancient Egypt measured time with a sun clock shaped like a bent T. The crossbar of the T stuck up. The long part of the T lay on the ground, and had marks drawn across it. As the crossbar's shadow moved along the marks, the priests could tell the hour of the day.

In the morning, the clock was placed with the crossbar toward the east. Then the sun would be behind it and the crossbar would cast a shadow. In the afternoon, the clock was turned around, with the crossbar toward the west, so that the sun would be behind it again.

People of long ago invented many kinds of sun clocks, or sundials. But the trouble with a sun clock, of course, is that it is no good at night or on a cloudy day. So people started looking for ways of measuring time that didn't depend on the sun.

Water clocks and sand clocks

Measuring time by the sun or the stars is all very well, but people soon needed a better way. And this need led to the invention of the water clock.

The first water clock was just a large clay or stone jar. Running down the inside was a row of marks for the hours. Near the bottom of the jar there was a tiny opening through which the water slowly leaked out. Of course, the amount of water that leaked out, and the space between the marks, had to be figured out very carefully. To tell the time, a person looked into the jar to see which mark was at the top of the water.

Although people still used sundials, water clocks were a better way of measuring time. Not only were the water clocks more accurate, but they could be used both day and night, rain or shine. In time, people found ways to make even better water clocks. They made water clocks that had dials, like our clocks of today. They even had water clocks that would ring a bell at the beginning of each hour.

Ancient Egyptians used this water clock about 3,300 years ago. The water ran out of a hole in the bottom. As the water in the pot sank lower, dots on the inside of the pot showed the hours.

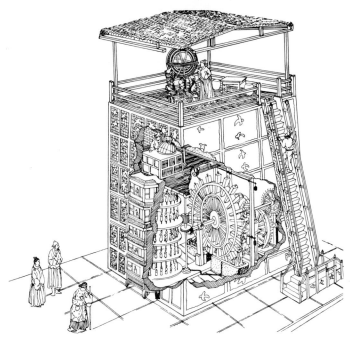

Chinese mathematicians built this marvelous water clock about nine hundred years ago. European clockmakers may have gotten many ideas for machinery from the Chinese.

The sand in a sand clock is carefully measured to run out of the top into the bottom in an exact amount of time, such as an hour, or even twenty-four hours.

But there were problems with water clocks just as there were with sundials. For one thing, a water clock was liable to freeze in very cold weather. For another thing, the hours marked off on water clocks were never quite the same. An hour on one water clock might be longer or shorter than an hour on another water clock. So people kept on looking for better ways to measure time.

About twelve hundred years ago, people in Europe began to use sand clocks, or what we call hourglasses. An hourglass is two glass bulbs connected together by a short, narrow tube. One of the bulbs is filled with fine sand, and the sand slowly drains out of the top bulb into the bottom one. The amount of sand is carefully measured so that it takes one hour to drain from one bulb to the other.

A sand clock works both day and night, in any kind of weather. But it only measures a given length of time, such as an hour or a half hour. It can't tell you what time it is.

Minutes, seconds, and nanoseconds

Atop a tower in the town square hung a big bell. At each side of the bell was a large iron statue of a man. Each statue held a hammer in its hands.

Suddenly, one of the statues seemed to come jerkily to life! It swung its arms, and the hammer struck the bell with a great, loud bong. Moments later, the second statue also moved. Its hammer bonged against the bell. Then, the two statues become stiff and motionless again. But the two bongs of the bell told everyone in the town that the time was two o'clock.

Until about three hundred years ago, people didn't have a need for clocks that measured anything other than hours. The clocks in most of Europe were just big machines that rang a bell so many times to announce the hour.

Perhaps this is how they came to be called clocks, for *clock* comes from an old word that means "bell." The first big clock that had a bell on which the hours were struck was made and set up in Milan, Italy, about 650 years ago.

As years passed, clocks were made with faces, and a hand that showed the hour. But there were no minute or second hands.

Then, about three hundred years ago, a man named Christian Huygens invented a clock that had a pendulum (PEN juh luhm). A pendulum is a long swinging weight that moves back and forth. With a pendulum, which swings at a steady, even pace, clocks could be made to keep time much more accurately. Today, many clocks, such as cuckoo clocks and grandfather clocks have a pendulum.

Many people, especially scientists, soon found that they needed smaller measurements of time than just hours. So, before long, clocks were made with faces divided into sixty spaces for minutes, and a hand to show the minutes. Later, still another hand was added to show seconds. This was the beginning of the clocks and watches we have now.

But today, we've divided time into smaller and smaller units. Some scientists even use a kind of clock that measures a very small period of time called a nanosecond. A nanosecond is one-billionth of a second. So, each time your clock or watch ticks off a second, a billion nanoseconds have gone by!

Measuring speed

The mighty Superman can move faster than a speeding bullet—but how fast is that? A tiny snail creeps along at what is called a "snail's pace"—but how slow is that?

There's an easy way to measure the speed of everything, from a creeping snail to a bullet fired from a rifle. To measure speed you have to know only two things—time and distance. You simply find out how much time it takes for something to move a certain distance.

Suppose you wanted to know how fast—or how slowly—a snail crawls. You'd need a watch, for the time. For the distance, you might use a ruler. You simply find out how long the snail takes to crawl the length of the ruler.

Let's say the snail takes 6 minutes to travel 12 inches (30 centimeters). By dividing the distance by the time, you'll find that the snail moves at a speed of 2 inches (5 centimeters) per minute. At this rate, it would take the snail 528 hours (twenty-two days) to travel one mile (1.6 kilometers)!

	DISTANCE	TIME
	1 mile (1.6 kilometers)	1 second
	55 miles (88 kilometers)	1 hour
	1 mile (1.6 kilometers)	4 minutes
	10 feet (3 meters)	1 hour

This is how all speed is measured—with time and distance. But the time may be in minutes, seconds, or hours. And the distance may be in feet, meters, miles, or kilometers.

For most things, speed is measured in miles or kilometers per hour. This is the way the speed of a car is measured. When the pointer of a car's speedometer is on the number thirty, it means the car is moving at a speed of thirty miles, or thirty kilometers, per hour. That is, at this speed the car could go a distance of thirty miles, or thirty kilometers, in one hour.

The speed of people running in a short race, such as a hundred-meter dash, is measured in seconds. The world record for one hundred meters (110 yards) is 9.9 seconds for men and 10.8 seconds for women. How fast do you think you can run this distance? If you want to find out, just measure the distance, get a friend with a stopwatch to time you, and see!

And how fast is Superman? Well, to move faster than a speeding bullet he might have to travel at the speed of more than five thousand feet (1,500 meters) per second!

DISTANCE TIME	RATE OF SPEED
$\frac{1}{1}$ $\left(\frac{1.6}{1}\right)$	1 mile per second (1.6 kilometers per second)
$\frac{55}{1}$ $\left(\frac{88}{1}\right)$	55 miles per hour (88 kilometers per hour)
$\frac{1}{4}$ $\left(\frac{1.6}{4}\right)$	$\frac{1}{4}$ mile per minute (0.4 kilometer per minute)
$\frac{10}{1}$ $\left(\frac{3}{1}\right)$	10 feet per hour (3 meters per hour)

Measuring temperature

For thousands of years, people judged the temperature by how they felt. To check the heat of an oven, cooks put a hand into the oven. If the weather felt cold, people put on more clothes.

Long, long ago, the Aborigines of Australia wore little, if any, clothing. If it was cold at night, they simply curled up with one or more of their dogs. According to a story which may or may not be true, these people "measured" the temperature by the number of dogs they needed to keep them warm! A "one-dog night" might be a little chilly. A "three-dog night" was, of course, much colder.

There was no way to *measure* temperature until the invention of the thermometer (thuhr

A Swedish astronomer, Anders Celsius, was the man who developed the Celsius system for measuring temperature.

MAHM uh tuhr) about four hundred years ago. And it wasn't until some 260 years ago that a German named Fahrenheit (FAR uhn hyt) built the kind of thermometer we use today. The word *thermometer* means "heat measure."

Fahrenheit's thermometer was a closed glass tube with a bulb at one end. The bulb was filled with mercury. When the mercury was warm, it would creep up the tube. When it was cool, it would drop back down toward the bulb.

To measure temperature, Fahrenheit needed a scale, or series of marks, on the glass tube. When he put the thermometer into a mixture of ice and salt, the mercury went nearly all the way down the tube. So, Fahrenheit put a mark on the tube at this place. He called this point zero degrees, or 0°.

Now he needed a high point. On some other temperature scales, the heat of the human body was marked at 12. But Fahrenheit had a very exact thermometer, and a scale of 0 to 12 was not great enough. So, he multiplied the 12 eight times and used 96 for his high point.

Using this scale, he found that the freezing point of water was 32 degrees. After extending the scale higher, he found that the boiling point of water was 212 degrees.

Today, people in most parts of the world use a thermometer that has a different scale. This scale, part of the metric system, is called the Celsius (SEHL see uhs) scale after the Swedish astronomer who worked it out. On the Celsius scale, 0 is the point at which water freezes. This is the same as 32 degrees on the Fahrenheit scale. And on the Celsius scale, the boiling point of water is 100 degrees. This is the same as 212 degrees on the Fahrenheit scale.

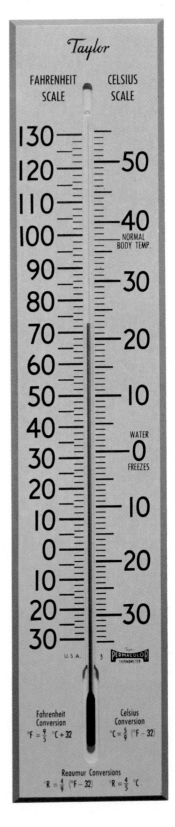

Measuring mountains

Have you ever wondered how people measure the height of a mountain? They don't do it by climbing the mountain and measuring with a ruler as they go! The height of a mountain is found by measuring angles.

Perhaps there are no mountains where you live, but there are certainly trees, flagpoles, lampposts and other tall things. Would you like to know how to use angles to find out how tall these things are?

First, you have to make a theodolite (thee AHD uh lyt), which is a tool for finding angles. Of course, your homemade theodolite will be a very simple one. People who actually measure the height of mountains and the size of large areas of land use a very complicated theodolite. Such a theodolite has a telescope, and number scales with which angles and distances can be measured. Even so, your theodolite will do the same basic job as theirs.

You will find it very easy to make your own theodolite. The things you will need to make it are listed below. The piece of cardboard should be fairly thick and at least six inches (15 centimeters) in length and width.

This is the kind of theodolite engineers and surveyors use to measure angles and distances.

What you will need
a piece of thick cardboard
a plastic or paper drinking straw
scissors
a small screw
a tape measure, yardstick,
    or meter stick
thread
transparent tape

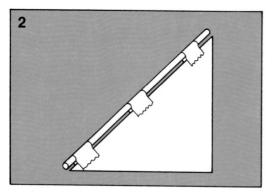

1 Cut the cardboard so that you have a square that measures about 6 inches (15 centimeters) on each side. Then, cut the square in half, slantwise, from one corner to the other, so that you have two right triangles.

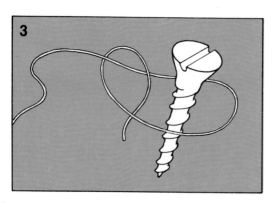

2 Using some pieces of transparent tape, fasten the straw along the long edge of one of the triangles.

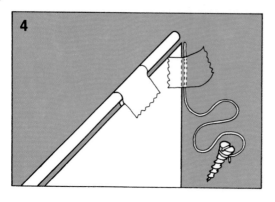

3 Cut off a piece of thread about 10 inches (25 centimeters) long. Tie the screw to one end of the thread.

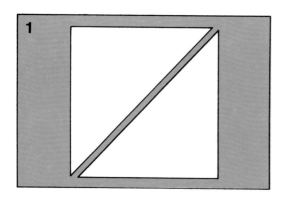

4 Using one or two pieces of transparent tape, fasten the other end of the thread under the top end of the straw, so that the thread hangs straight down along the edge of the triangle.

To use the theodolite, pick out a tall object such as a tree, or building, or flagpole. Raise the theodolite to your eye. Hold the theodolite so that the thread hangs straight down along the edge of the cardboard triangle. If it hangs away from the triangle, either to the front or to the side, move the triangle until the thread hangs straight down the edge of the triangle.

Looking through the straw, and keeping the thread straight, move backward or forward until you can see the very top of the object you want to measure.

From where you are, an imaginary line stretches on an angle from your eye to the top of the object you're measuring. Another imaginary line, this one level, goes from your eye to the object.

These imaginary lines form an angle. Your cardboard theodolite has a fixed angle of 45 degrees because of its shape. This is why you don't have to measure the angle.

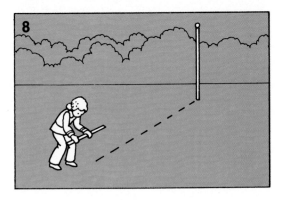

All you have to do now is use the tape measure, or measuring stick, to measure the distance from where you are standing to the bottom of the object you are looking at. To this distance, you have to add your height. The total of these two numbers is the height of the object you're measuring— whether it's a tree or a mountain!

If the object you are measuring is 45 feet away, and you are five feet tall, you know that the object is 50 feet high.

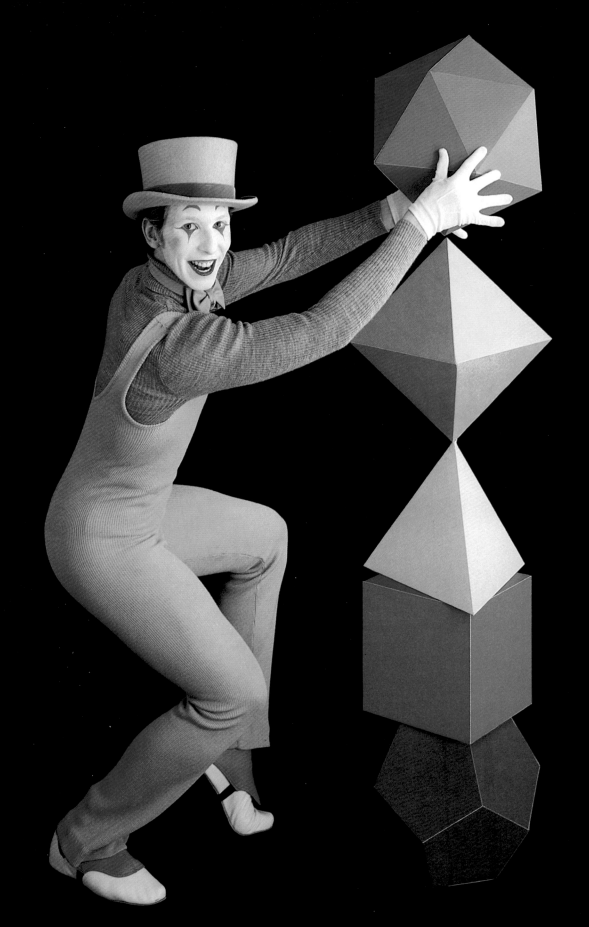

7

Points, lines, shapes, and designs

Start with two points.
Connect them with a line.
Then make an angle
(You're doing fine).
Close the angle
And a triangle's there.
Put two triangles together
—You've got a square!
And squares and triangles
And points and lines
Are the things we use
To make shapes and designs!

Shapes everywhere

angles

rectangle

square

triangle

octagon

circle

cylinder

disk

sphere

cone

cube

Just as you live in a world of numbers, you also live in a world of shapes.

Your house or apartment is full of shapes. Every corner forms a shape called an angle. Every door and doorway is a shape called a rectangle. Most windows are rectangles, too, and often they're divided into smaller rectangles.

If you live in an apartment, the building probably has a flat roof. But if you live in a house, chances are that the ends of the roof form a shape called a triangle.

Concrete sidewalks are divided into shapes called squares or rectangles. The lines that separate the squares or rectangles are shapes, too, because a line is a shape. A stop sign on the street corner is an eight-sided shape called an octagon. A manhole cover on the street looks like a round, flat shape called a circle. But, because it has thickness, it is really a round, solid shape called a disk. And most coins are also disks.

Did you ever blow soap bubbles? Round, gleaming soap bubbles that float in the air are shapes called spheres. So are baseballs, tennis balls, basketballs, and globes.

A tin can is a shape called a cylinder. And a telephone pole is a cylinder, too.

An ice-cream cone is named for its shape, which is a cone. Ice cubes and sugar cubes are also named for their shape, the cube.

As you can see, you really do live in a world of shapes! So let's take a look at some of the many kinds of shapes around us.

Points and lines

What is this · ?

You probably said, "It's a dot." Or maybe you said, "It's a period." Well, it could be a dot or a period. But to mathematicians, it's a picture of a point.

You probably think of a point as the sharp tip of a needle or a pin. But to mathematicians, a point is a place. When you say to a friend, "I'll see you down at the corner," you mean a place where two streets meet. A mathematician might talk about a place by saying, "It is at the point where the two lines cross."

If you look at the point where the two lines cross, you won't see anything. That's because a point is invisible. It's just an idea. A point has no length, or width, or thickness. Because we can't measure a point, we say that a point has no dimensions. But to show where a point is, we often put a dot there. So the picture of a point does have some size and shape.

You can't see or measure a point. But when you have a lot of these invisible points in a row, all touching each other, they make something that you can see and measure. They make a line! At least that's the way mathematicians think of a line—as a row of points.

Now, a line has length, doesn't it? You can measure the length of a line with a ruler. So a line has one dimension, length. Mathematicians think of a line as having no width or thickness. Of course, we can't draw it this way. Even the finest line you can draw has some width.

None of this seems very important, does it? But it is! You see, every line is made up of a great many points. And every shape—triangles, squares, circles—is made up of lines. So, points and lines are the things we use to make designs. Without them, we couldn't make any designs.

GET YOUR
SOUVENIR POINT

This
is
IT

DON'T MISS
THE
POINT

This way
to the
POINT

SEE THE
Mathematician's
MAGIC POINT

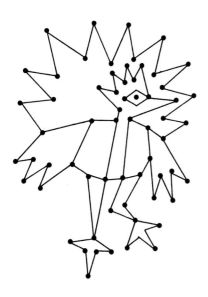

Dot-picture shapes.

You've probably made dot pictures lots of times. They're pictures you make by drawing lines from one dot to another. Well, here are some special dot pictures you can make for yourself.

Get a paper and pencil and make three dots, or points, like this:

Draw a line between two of the dots. Then draw another line to the third dot, like this:

You have made a picture. But a picture of what?

The picture you've made is a shape called an angle (ANG guhl). As you can see, it's a kind of corner. Whenever two lines come together at a point, they make an angle. No matter where you put your three dots, the lines you draw between the dots will always make some kind of angle. Try it and see!

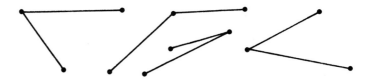

As you can see, angles are very important in making designs of all kinds.

Meet the angle family

People have names. And we give names to different kinds of animals. So why shouldn't angles have names?

They do! Angles are named after the kind of corner they make.

An angle that forms a square corner is called a right angle. That's easy to remember. All you have to do is think about how two of these angles are just right for making a square!

An angle that is less than a right angle is called an acute (uh KYOOT) angle. *Acute* means "sharp." And, as you can see, an acute angle is a rather sharp shape.

An angle that is greater than a right angle is called an obtuse (uhb TOOS) angle. *Obtuse* means "blunt." And, as you can see, an obtuse angle is a rather blunt shape.

There is one other kind of angle—one that may come as a surprise to you. It's called a straight angle, and it looks like this:

But, you say, that's not an angle. It doesn't make a corner. No, it doesn't make a corner. But it's still an angle. That's because whenever two lines come together at a point, they make an angle. So, believe it or not, this is an angle.

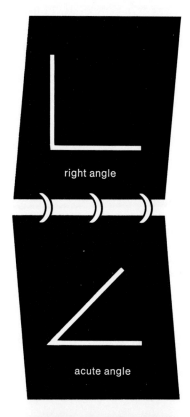

right angle

acute angle

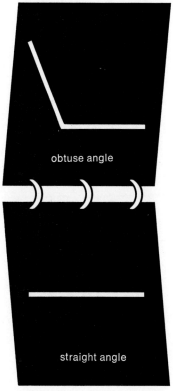

obtuse angle

straight angle

Meet the triangle family

Every angle has one side that is open. If you close this open side, you'll have a closed shape with three straight sides and three angles.

A shape of this kind is called a triangle (TRY ang guhl). *Triangle* means "three angles."

If a triangle could talk, it might say that it's "better" than either a point or a line. A point, remember, has no dimensions. A line has one dimension—length. But a triangle (or any other closed shape, such as a square or circle), has two dimensions—length and width. You can measure a triangle's sides to find out how long they are. And you can measure the distance from one side to another side to find out how wide a triangle is.

Just as there are different kinds of angles, there are different kinds of triangles. And just as angles have special names, so do triangles.

Some triangles are named after the kinds of angles they have.

For example, an angle that makes a square corner is called a right angle. And a triangle with a right angle in it is called a right triangle.

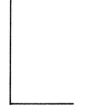

An angle that is less than a right angle is called an acute angle. And a triangle with three acute angles is called an acute triangle.

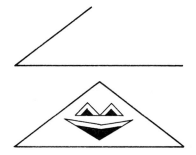

An angle that is greater than a right angle is called an obtuse angle. And a triangle with one obtuse angle is called an obtuse triangle.

Other kinds of triangles have special names that describe the way they look.

A triangle that has two sides, or "legs," that are equal in length, and two equal angles at the base, is called an isosceles (eye SAHS uh leez) triangle. *Isosceles* means "equal legs."

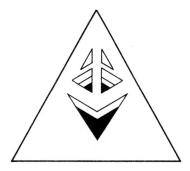

A triangle that has three sides that are equal in length, and three equal angles, is called an equilateral (ee kwuh LAT uhr uhl) triangle. The word *equilateral* means "equal sides."

A triangle that has sides of three different lengths, and three unequal angles, is called a scalene (skay LEEN) triangle. The word *scalene* means "uneven legs."

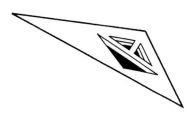

A triangular tale

A triangle called Isosceles,
And his friend who was known as Obtuse,
Were arguing over the very best way
To cook a Christmas goose.

"Let's bake it," the Obtuse one said,
"In an open fireplace,
Equilaterally sprinkled
With sage, rosemary, and mace."

"What nonsense!" said Isosceles.
"I wish you were more Acute!
If we do it the way that you suggest,
It will soon be covered with soot!"

"Then boil it," said the Obtuse one,
"In water that's bubbly hot,
Right on top of the kitchen stove
In a lovely Triangular pot!"

"Gracious, Obtuse, but you are dull,"
Isosceles said with a sneer.
"Why, the only way to cook a goose
Is to roast it, do you hear?"

And while they argued to make their points,
And each angled to get his way,
A Scalene thief with one short leg
Came and stole the goose away!

Triangle tricks

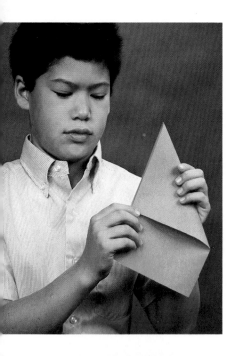

Triangles are tricky shapes. You can do some surprising things with them.

Let's make a triangle that you can do some tricks with. You'll need a piece of paper about the size of this book, and a scissors.

First, fold the paper in half by bringing the top edge down to the bottom edge. Now, with the folded edge at the top, take the upper left-hand corner and fold it slantwise toward you, so that the corner is even with the bottom edge of the paper. Crease the fold. Now, unfold the paper. With the scissors, cut along the fold marks that form the large triangle.

This one triangle is really two different kinds of triangles. You can see the two triangles more easily if you move the paper triangle around. Put the longest side at the bottom and you'll see that the two "legs" are the same length. So, you have the kind of triangle called an isosceles triangle. Now move the triangle around until one of the "legs" is at the bottom. You'll see that one of the angles at the bottom is a right angle. So, you also have a right triangle.

isosceles triangle

right triangle

Cut your triangle in half, along the fold line. Now you have two triangles, each one shaped exactly the same as the big one you had before.

Place the two triangles side by side, with the long side at the bottom.

Turn one triangle around until the long side is at the top. Now slide the two triangles together.

The two triangles now form a shape called a parallelogram (par uh LEHL uh gram). Look at this shape carefully. You'll see that the sides that are across from each other are the same length. These sides are also parallel—that is, they are the same distance apart at all points. (You can measure them and see.)

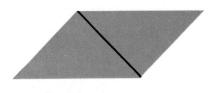

parallelogram

Next, move one triangle around until the right angle is at the lower left. Move the other triangle until the right angle is at the lower right.

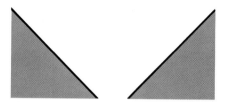

Now, turn one triangle so that its long side fits against the long side of the other. What shape do you have now?

A square, of course! To be a square, a shape must have four right angles and four sides that are all the same length.

square

Fold each of the two triangles in half and cut along the fold lines. With a little practice, you will find that you can fit these four triangles together to make many shapes and designs.

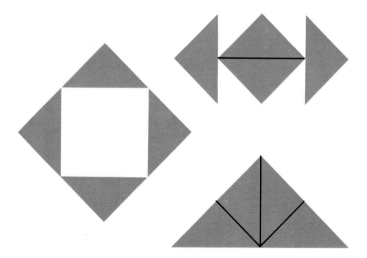

Then, cut each of the four triangles in half again, so that you have eight triangles. You'll find that you can now make quite different shapes and designs.

Here are a few of the ways in which you can put triangles together to make interesting shapes and designs.

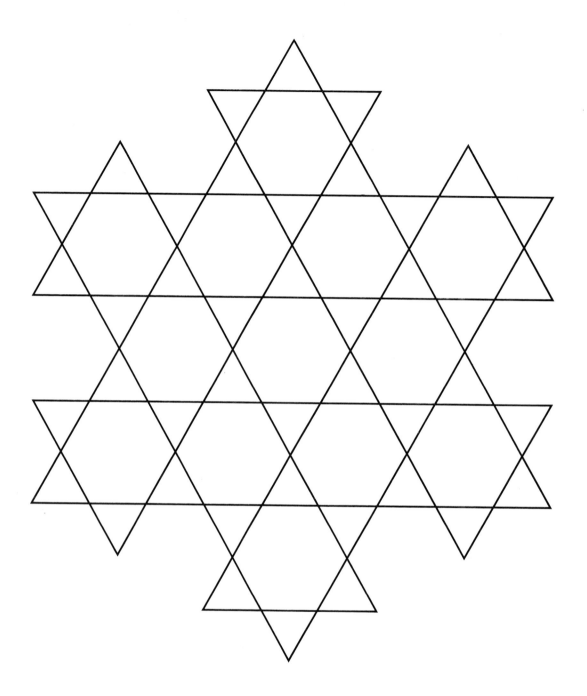

Counting triangles

The design shown above is made entirely of triangles. How many triangles, of all sizes, do you think there are? Altogether, there are 87 triangles! See if you can find them all.

There are 41 triangles of this size, pointing in all directions.

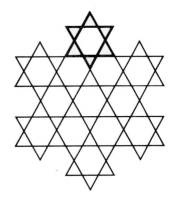

There are 26 triangles of this size, 13 pointing up and 13 pointing down.

There are 12 triangles of this size, 6 pointing up and 6 pointing down.

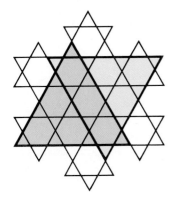

There are 6 triangles of this size, 3 pointing up and 3 pointing down.

And there are 2 triangles of this size, 1 pointing up and 1 pointing down.

That makes 87 triangles altogether. Did you find them all? Or did you get dizzy before you finished?

A square puzzle

Long ago, there was a farmer whose land was in the shape of a square. Each side of the square was exactly one hundred paces long.

One day, a tired, dusty man knocked on the farmer's door and asked for something to eat. The farmer, being a kind person, gave the man a nice lunch.

After the man had eaten, he said, "Farmer, I am your king! As a reward for your kindness in giving me food when you thought I was just a humble stranger, you may double the size of your land. But when you have added the new land, your farm must still be in the shape of a square!"

The farmer was overjoyed, for now he could plant twice as many crops. He went out at once to measure his new land so that he could put a fence around it. But he suddenly found that he had a problem.

At first, the doubling of his square of land seemed easy. Since each side of the square was one hundred paces long, it seemed as if the sides of the new square should be two hundred paces long—twice the length of the old sides. But this didn't work. His new square, with sides two hundred paces long, wasn't twice as big as the old square—it was four times as big! In fact, it contained as much land as four squares with sides one hundred paces long!

The farmer scratched his head. Finally, he went back to his house and got out paper and pencil. He thought long and hard. Then he had an idea. He would divide his square of land into four small squares. Then he could simply add on four new squares the same size as the small ones. This way he'd have exactly twice the amount of land that was in the old square.

First, he tried adding all the small squares onto one side of his old square. But this was no good. It gave him a rectangle, not a square.

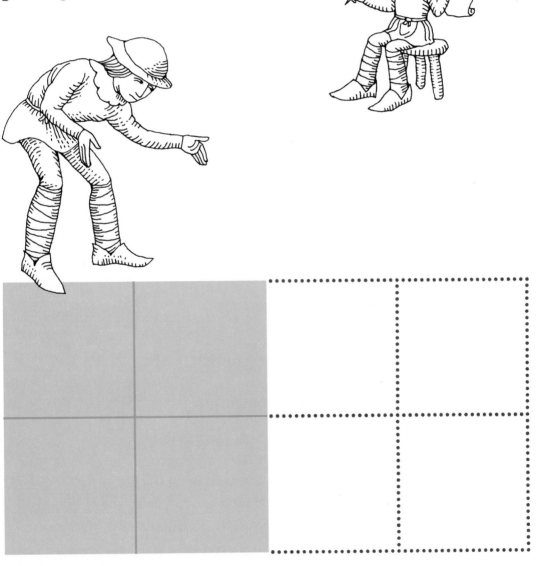

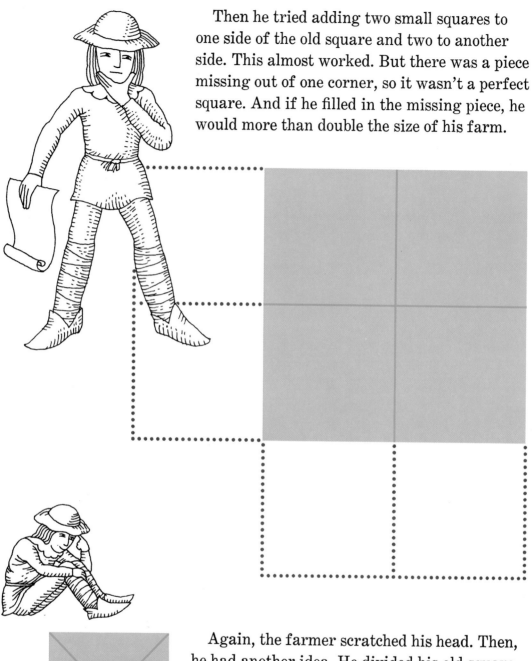

Then he tried adding two small squares to one side of the old square and two to another side. This almost worked. But there was a piece missing out of one corner, so it wasn't a perfect square. And if he filled in the missing piece, he would more than double the size of his farm.

Again, the farmer scratched his head. Then, he had another idea. He divided his old square into four parts by drawing diagonal lines between the opposite corners. Now the square was divided into four triangles. If he could add four more triangles of exactly the same size—and somehow make a square—he would have solved the puzzle!

So he added a triangle to one side of the old square.

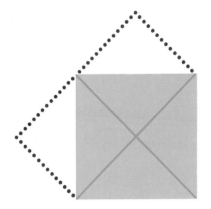

Then he added a triangle to another side.

Then he put triangles on each of the other sides.

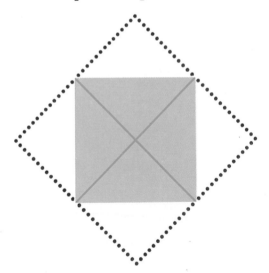

This made a diamond shape. But when he turned the diamond on its side, he saw that it was a square! He had solved his puzzle.

And that's the way you double the size of a square and still have a square!

The "magic" triangle

Thousands of years ago, in ancient Egypt, there were men known as "rope-stretchers." It was their job to mark out the boundaries of fields and the foundations for houses, temples, and palaces.

The ancient Egyptians preferred square and rectangular fields and buildings, with perfectly

square corners. But they didn't have all the special measuring tools we have today. So how do you suppose the rope-stretchers were able to make perfectly square corners? Well, they did it with a "magic" triangle.

To make a square corner, the rope-stretchers used a long piece of rope tied into a loop. Tied in the rope were twelve equally spaced knots, just like the marks on a ruler.

First the rope-stretchers pounded a stake into the ground where they wanted a corner. They placed one of the knots at this stake. Then they counted out three knots and pulled the rope tight. Another stake was pounded into the ground at the third knot.

Going back to the corner stake, they picked up the other part of the rope and counted out four knots. Holding the fourth knot, they pulled the rope so that all the sides were tight. Then they pounded a stake into place at the fourth knot. And, presto, they had a "magic" triangle with the square corner they needed for a field or a building.

What the rope-stretchers had done was make a right triangle—a triangle that has one right angle forming a square corner. The trick, of course, was in knowing which knots to put the stakes at. There were twelve knots in the loop of rope. So there were also twelve equal spaces.

On one side of the corner, the stretched-out rope had three spaces. On the other side, it had four spaces. And on the side opposite the corner there were five spaces. So the sides of the triangle were three, four, and five spaces long. And anytime you have a triangle with sides having this three, four, five relationship, it will *always* be a right triangle.

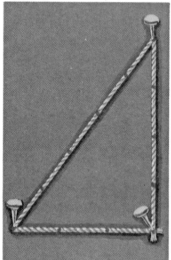

Try it yourself and see. Cut a length of string and make thirteen equally spaced marks on it. Put the two end marks on top of one another and push a tack through both marks so that the string forms a loop. You will now have a loop of string with 12 equal spaces. Push the tack into a piece of wood or heavy cardboard. This will be your corner.

Count out three marks from the corner. Push a tack through this mark. Pull the string tight and fasten it to the board. Go back to the corner tack and count out four marks. Push a tack through this mark. Pull the string until all three sides are tight. Fasten the tack at the fourth mark to the board. You now have a "magic" triangle just like the one made by the Egyptian rope-stretchers!

The Egyptian rope-stretchers weren't the only ones who knew how to make a right triangle. People in other parts of the world also knew the secret. And, in time, some people began to wonder just why this way of making a right triangle always worked.

One of the people who wondered about this was an ancient Greek named Pythagoras (pih THAG uh ruhs). Pythagoras made dozens and dozens of right triangles of different sizes. And when he *squared* the sides of the triangles he discovered something very interesting. What he learned can be shown in picture form, like this:

To square a number, multiply the number by itself. The triangle in the picture has sides 3, 4, and 5 units long. When you multiply 5 × 5, you get 25. Then you multiply 4 × 4, getting 16, and 3 × 3, getting 9. Count the little squares next to each of the triangle's sides and you'll see that there are 25, 16, and 9 of them.

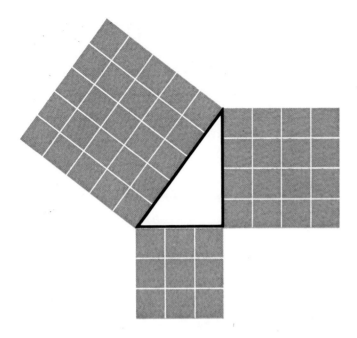

Now if you add the numbers you got by
squaring the two smallest sides—9 and 16—
you get 25. So, the number of little squares
next to the two short sides of the triangle add
up to the *same amount* as the number of
squares next to the longest side!

Pythagoras made up a rule about this. The
rule says that for a right triangle the square of
the longest side equals the sum of the squares
of the other two sides. The longest side has a
special name. It is called the *hypotenuse* (hy
PAHT uh noos), which means "stretching under."

This is something that is true of all right
triangles. It is why Egyptian rope-stretchers
always got a right triangle with their knotted
rope. As long as they staked out triangles with
sides having a three, four, five relationship,
they could *only* get a right triangle.

What Pythagoras learned may not seem very
important, but it is. His rule helps engineers,
mathematicians, astronomers, and others to
solve many different kinds of problems.

The magical shape

Do you belong to a club that has a secret password or a secret symbol? Some twenty-five hundred years ago, in ancient Greece, there was a kind of club called The Brotherhood.

This "club" was really a school run by the Greek mathematician Pythagoras. All of the young men who went to the school studied mathematics, magic, and religion. They took an oath never to reveal the mathematical secrets they learned. The penalty for giving away a secret was death!

All the members of The Brotherhood wore a symbol that looked like this:

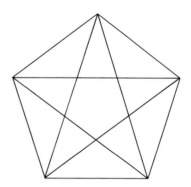

This shape is called a pentagon (PEHN tuh gahn), which means "five angles." Inside the pentagon is another shape, a five-pointed star called a pentagram (PEHN tuh gram). If you look closely, you'll see that in the middle of the star there is a small pentagon.

The thing that was secret about this symbol was that nobody else knew how to make it. (If you think it is easy, try it.) Only the members of The Brotherhood knew how to do it.

They had learned how to make solid shapes, such as cubes and pyramids, by putting together flat shapes such as squares and triangles. One shape they made was a five-sided pyramid made of five same-sized equilateral triangles. The *bottom* of such a shape is a pentagon! To get their secret symbol, they traced around the bottom of the shape. Then they drew diagonal lines from each of the corners. This made a pentagram with a small pentagon in the middle.

Because the pentagon and pentagram were secret shapes, a lot of people thought there was

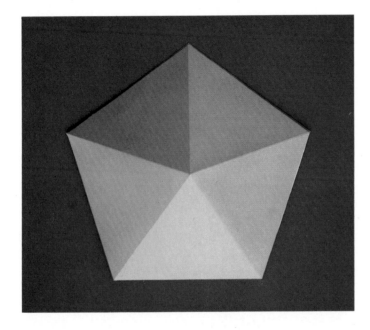

Five equal-sided triangles will fit together to make a solid shape—one with length, width, and thickness. The bottom of this shape forms a five-sided shape called a pentagon.

something magical about them. Many years later, when The Brotherhood was no more, people believed it had been a secret society of magicians. And they thought the pentagram, or five-pointed star, had been one of its greatest magical tools!

For hundreds of years, people who wanted to be witches or wizards used drawings of pentagrams whenever they tried to cast their magic spells!

Snowflakes
and honeybees

Snowflakes are a beautiful sight as they come spinning down out of the sky on a gray winter day. But they are even more beautiful when you see them close up, through a microscope. Then, they look like the work of an artist. You can see that each snowflake has a lovely, lacy design. And each design is different!

Even though the design of every snowflake is different, the shape of every snowflake is the same. It is always a shape with six sides—a shape called a hexagon (HEHK suh gahn).

A hexagon is made of six equilateral, or equal-sided, triangles. Lots of things around us have the shape of a hexagon. Most insects

These are snowflakes seen through a microscope. Each of them is a six-sided shape called a hexagon.

have eyes that are made up of a great many tiny hexagons. To the insects, things probably appear to be broken up into hexagons.

Honeybees make their honeycombs, or storage chambers for honey, in the shape of hexagons. Some wasps and other insects also make hexagon-shaped storage chambers in their nests. And this is really the very best shape these insects could use, because hexagons fit together perfectly.

In fact, there are only three shapes—triangles, squares, and hexagons—that will fit together perfectly on all sides. If you wanted to cover a tabletop with tiles, you could do it using triangles, or squares, or hexagons of the same size and there wouldn't be any gaps between the tiles. But you couldn't do it with any other shape! There would be gaps between the tiles.

Bees make hexagon-shaped compartments to store their honey in. The hexagons fit together perfectly, forming what we call a honeycomb.

A thousand and one hexagons

Have you ever looked into a kaleidoscope
(kuh LY duh skohp)? A kaleidoscope is a toy
that makes beautiful designs—thousands and
thousands of different designs.

You can make a kaleidoscope for yourself
very easily, and it will give you hours of fun.
This kind of kaleidoscope will make designs
like snowflakes, in the shape of a hexagon.

What you will need:
three small, two-sided mirrors, each about
    2x3 inches (5x8 centimeters). Two-sided
    mirrors work best because there is no
    trim that will keep the edges apart
transparent tape
white glue
stiff white paper
scraps of different colored paper
scissors

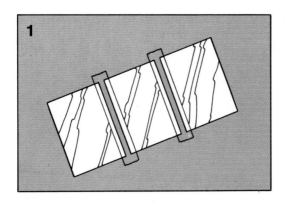

Place the three mirrors on a flat surface. The long edges should be next to each other, but not quite touching. Cut a length of transparent tape about as long as the long edge of one mirror. Press the tape down firmly so that it holds the edges of two of the mirrors together. But be sure to keep the space between the mirrors. Cut another length of tape and fasten the other two mirrors together.

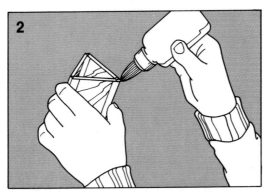

Stand the mirrors up. Keeping the taped sides out, fold the two outside mirrors toward each other. Cut another piece of tape and tape the last two edges together. Use the scissors to trim off any tape that sticks up at the top or bottom.

Put a small amount of white glue on the top edges of the mirrors. Don't use too much glue.

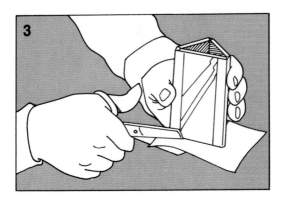

Set the glued edges on the piece of stiff white paper. After the glue is dry, trim off any of the paper that sticks out past the edges of the mirrors. One end of your kaleidoscope is now closed.

Cut the scraps of colored paper into tiny shapes—triangles, squares, strips, and so on. Make the shapes as small as you can. The more shapes you have, the better. Drop these paper shapes into the kaleidoscope.

Hold the kaleidoscope so that one of the taped edges is pointed toward your chest. Tilt the kaleidoscope slightly and tap the sides so that all the bits of paper collect in the corner facing you. Hold the kaleidoscope close to one eye and look straight down into it. You'll see a lovely six-sided design. You can change the design by turning the kaleidoscope and getting the bits of paper into another corner.

You see a six-sided shape because you see the corner with the colored paper plus five reflections. The result is a hexagon.

Stonehenge, a large circle of tall stones, was made by ancient people of England.

The circle of stones

About four thousand years ago, a group of men gathered together on a broad, green plain in what is now southern England. With a stone hammer, one of the men pounded a wooden stake into the ground. Then he tied a very long leather line to the stake. Another man took hold of the line and walked away from the stake until the line was stretched out tight.

Keeping the line stretched tight, this man began to walk around the stake. He stopped after each step, while another man put a small, white pebble by his foot. When the man with the line had walked all the way around the stake, there was a perfect circle of pebbles.

After they had marked out the circle, the men began to dig a circular ditch and pile up a circle of earth. Later, rings of huge, rectangular stone blocks were set up inside the circle. It took some four hundred years to complete the job of building this huge, circular monument.

Today, many of the big stones have fallen over and others are missing. But a number still stand, showing us what the ring of stones must have looked like long ago. We call this ancient monument Stonehenge, or "hanging stones."

radius

Most scientists think that Stonehenge was a kind of giant calendar and observatory. The people of long ago may have used it to follow the movements of the sun and the moon, and even to predict eclipses. In this way, they would have been able to keep track of special days that were holy for them.

The prehistoric people who built Stonehenge used the oldest way known to make a circle. You can make circles the same way, using a string with one end tied to a tack and the other end tied to a pencil. By keeping the string tight, and moving the pencil all the way around the tack, you can draw a perfect circle.

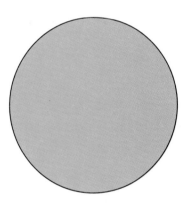

circumference

Doing this also tells you something about a circle—that every point on the line that forms a circle is the same distance from the center. This distance is called the radius (RAY dee uhs). The distance around a circle is called the circumference (suhr KUHM fuhr uhns). And the distance across a circle, going through the center, is called the diameter (dy AM uh tuhr).

diameter

The Roads of Math

Take a line, a straight line,
   And divide it into three.
Make the three lines form three angles,
   And a triangle have we.

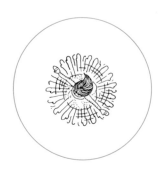
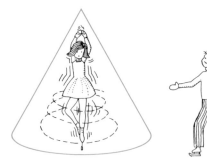

Now take this little triangle
   And twirl it about in space.
Twirl the triangle 'round and 'round;
   A cone is what we face.

Now look at the bottom of our cone.
   We see a circle true.
Now let's examine the circle
   And what it can do for you.

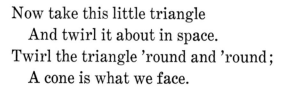

Let's draw a line through the center
   Of our circle round.
We've discovered something new:
   The diameter we've found.

Let's look at the line 'round the circle.
   The circumference says, "Hi!"
Divide the circumference by the diameter,
   And we've found the number Pi.[1]

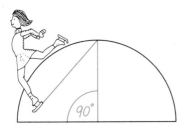

Now take our semicircle
    And take a point on the rim.
Using the diameter, form a triangle.
    (It doesn't take much vim.)

Look carefully at this triangle.
    If you do, something different you'll see,
For the largest of its angles
    Has exactly ninety degrees.

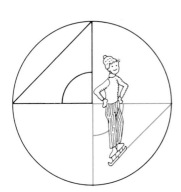

Now take two of these new right angles.
    Put their vertices[2] in the circle's center, there.
With the diameter under one side of each angle,
    We're ready to form a square.

Mark the points on the circumference
    Where the right angles do fall.
Construct triangles in both semicircles,
    And that is all.

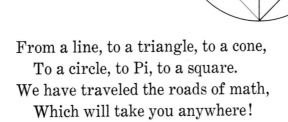

From a line, to a triangle, to a cone,
    To a circle, to Pi, to a square.
We have traveled the roads of math,
    Which will take you anywhere!

Jeffrey Dielle

---

[1] Pi is a Greek letter that looks like this π. In mathematics, Pi is a symbol for a number close to 3.14. To find the circumference of a circle, multiply the diameter by 3.14. And, as the poem says, if you divide the circumference by the diameter, you get the number 3.14.
[2] Vertices (VUR tuh seez) is the plural of vertex. The vertex is the point at which the sides of an angle come together.

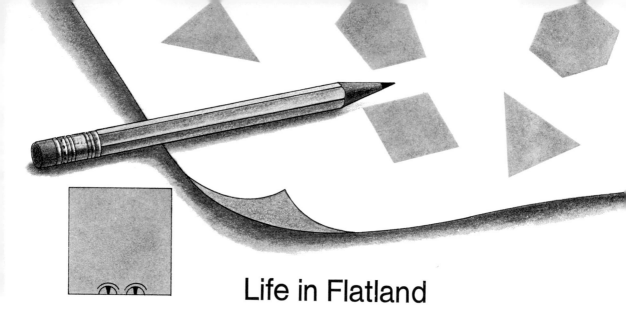

Life in Flatland

Adapted from *Flatland*
by A. Square

Flatland is the story of a very strange place in which all of the people are Triangles, Squares, Circles, and other flat shapes. The story is told by one of them, A. Square, who describes his country and tells about life there.

I call our world Flatland—not because this is what we call it, but so that you will know what it is like. You must understand at once that in my country there is nothing of the kind you call a solid shape. As you know, a solid, or three-dimensional shape, has length, width, and thickness. But in Flatland, *everything* is flat. That is, there are only two dimensions—length and width.

Imagine a huge sheet of paper on which Straight Lines, Triangles, Squares, Pentagons, Hexagons, and other shapes move freely about, very much like shadows. You will then have a pretty correct idea of what my country and countrymen look like. You might think that we can tell Triangles, Squares, and other flat shapes by sight. But this is not so. We cannot tell one shape from another. We can see only Straight Lines. Let me show you why this is so.

Place a penny in the middle of a table. Now, lean over the table and look straight down upon the penny. It will appear to be a Circle.

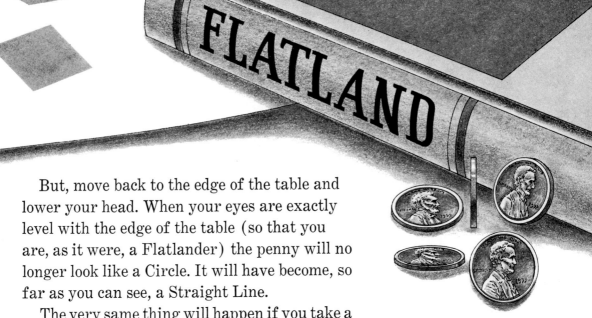

But, move back to the edge of the table and
lower your head. When your eyes are exactly
level with the edge of the table (so that you
are, as it were, a Flatlander) the penny will no
longer look like a Circle. It will have become, so
far as you can see, a Straight Line.

The very same thing will happen if you take a
piece of cardboard and cut out a Triangle, or
Square, or any other shape. Put the shape on a
table and look at it from the edge of the table.
You will find that you see only a Straight Line.

Well, that is exactly what we see in Flatland
when we meet a friend. As our friend comes
ever closer to us, the line becomes larger and
brighter. When our friend goes away from us,
the line becomes smaller and dimmer. Our
friend may be a Triangle, Square, Pentagon,
Hexagon, or any other shape, but all we see is
a Straight Line.

You may wonder how we can tell one friend
from another. I will explain in a moment. But
first, let me now tell you about the kinds of
people there are in Flatland.

Our Soldiers are Straight Lines. I shall have
more to say about them shortly.

All our Farmers are Isosceles Triangles, with
two equal sides, each about eleven inches (27
centimeters) long. The third side is quite short,
often not much more than half an inch (12
millimeters). This causes the two equal sides to

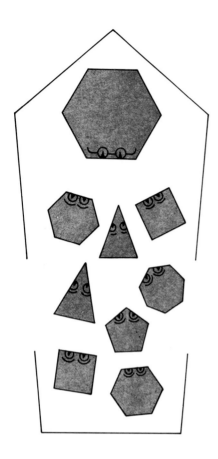

form a very sharp angle that is most useful for plowing.

Our Merchants and Shopkeepers, of whom there are many, are Equilateral, or Equal-Sided, Triangles.

Most of our fine Doctors and Lawyers are Squares, like myself. But a few, who have risen to the top of their profession, are Five-Sided shapes, or Pentagons.

There are several degrees of School Teachers, beginning with Six-Sided shapes, or Hexagons, and going on to shapes that have many more sides. Finally, we have our Philosophers, who are the wisest of all our people. They have so many sides, and the sides are so small, that these Flatlanders cannot be told from a Circle.

There are many dangers in Flatland, just as there are in your world. The greatest of these dangers is our shapes. We have to be careful not to bump into one another. A Flatlander who has a sharp shape can easily hurt another person. For this reason, our sharply pointed Farmer Triangles are quite dangerous.

This being so, you can see that our Soldiers are far more dangerous. If a Farmer is like an arrowhead, a Soldier is like a needle, inasmuch as a Soldier is all point (for a line, as you know, is made up entirely of points). Add to this the power Soldiers have of making themselves almost invisible and you can easily see that a Soldier of Flatland is not a person to trifle with!

Perhaps you are wondering how our Soldiers can make themselves invisible. Let me explain.

Place a needle on a table. Then, with your eye at the edge of the table, look at the needle sideways. You will see the whole length of it. But look at it end-ways and you see nothing but a point. It has become practically invisible. This is how it is with all of our Soldiers. When a Soldier's side is turned toward us, we see a Straight Line. When the end containing the Soldier's eye faces us, we see nothing but a rather gleaming point. But when a Soldier's back is to us, it is a dim point that is almost impossible to see.

You can understand, then, how dangerous our Soldiers are. You can get a gash by running into a Merchant Triangle. And you can be quite badly wounded in a collision with a Farmer Triangle. But it is nothing less than absolute death to bump into a Soldier! And when a Soldier is seen only as a dim point, it is difficult, even for the most cautious, to avoid a collision!

For this reason, our Soldiers must be careful. When any Soldiers are out in the street, either standing or walking about, they must move their backs constantly from side to side so that anyone behind them will be able to see them.

You lucky people who live in a world of three dimensions are blessed with shade as well as light. You enjoy many colors. You can see an angle and the complete shape of a Circle. But in Flatland, we do not have these blessings. How, then, can I make you understand the difficulty we have recognizing one another?

The first means of recognition is the sense of hearing. Our hearing is keener and more highly developed than is yours. It enables us not only to tell the voices of our friends, but even to tell the difference between shapes, at least for the Triangle, the Square, and the Pentagon.

But feeling is the best way of recognizing another Flatlander. What an "introduction" is to you, feeling is with us. "Permit me to ask

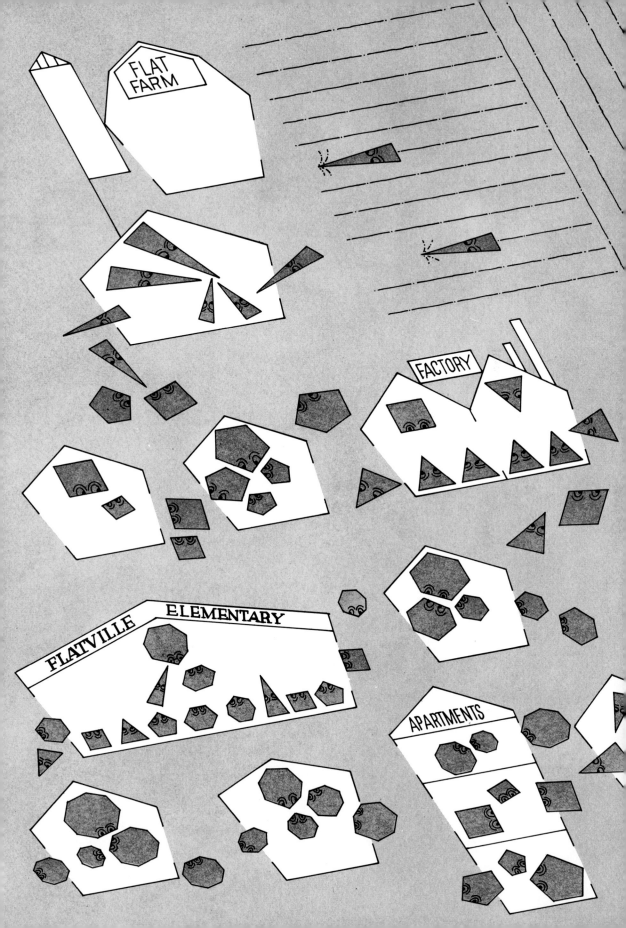

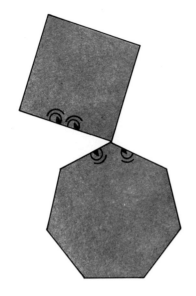

you to feel and be felt by my old friend Mr. So and So," is the way we introduce people to one another in Flatland.

However, you must not think that feeling is as slow and difficult for us as it might be for you. Long practice and training, which begins in school and goes on throughout life, make it possible for us to quickly tell the difference between the angles of an Equal-Sided Triangle, a Square, or a Pentagon.

It is not necessary, as a rule, to do more than feel a single angle to tell a person's shape, unless he or she belongs to the higher class of shapes. That makes it much more difficult. Even the professors in our University of Wentbridge have been known to confuse a Ten-Sided Polygon with a Twelve-Sided one. And there is hardly a Doctor of Science anywhere in Flatland who would know at once, just by feeling a single angle, the difference between a Twenty-Sided and a Twenty-Four-Sided shape.

Many of us prefer still a third method, which is recognition by the sense of sight.

That this power exists anywhere, and for any class, is the result of Fog. For Fog is present everywhere during most of the year, except in the very hot parts of Flatland. For you, Fog is a bad thing that hides the landscape, makes you feel poorly, and damages your health. But for us, Fog is a blessing, nearly as important as the air itself!

If there were no Fog, all our friends would look like exactly the same kind of Straight Line. But wherever there is a rich supply of Fog, an object only slightly farther away than another is a bit dimmer than the nearer object. So, by carefully examining the dimness and brightness of things, we are able to tell the exact shape of an object.

For example, suppose I were to see two people coming toward me. Let us say that one is a Merchant (an Equilateral Triangle) and the other is a Doctor (a Pentagon). Both appear to be Straight Lines, so how am I to tell one from the other? If you look at the picture, I think you will understand.

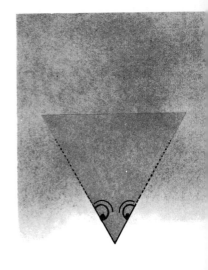

In the case of the Merchant, I see a Straight Line, of course. The center of this line, which is the part nearest to me, is very bright. But on either side, the line fades away rapidly into the Fog. I can tell at once, then, that the line slants back quite sharply from the center.

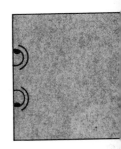

On the other hand, the Doctor has a slightly different appearance. As with the Merchant, I see only a Straight Line with a very bright center. On either side, the Doctor's line also fades into the Fog, but not as rapidly as the Merchant's line. Thus I can tell at once that the Doctor's line does not slant back as sharply. Because of the slight difference in brightness, I know that one shape is an Equilateral Triangle and that the other is a Pentagon.

But enough about how we recognize one another. Let me now say a word or two about our climate and our houses.

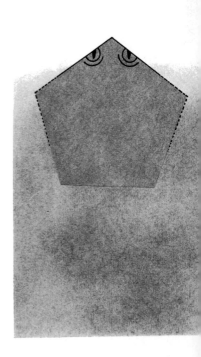

Just as you do, we have four points of the compass: North, South, East, and West. But because there is no sun—or, indeed, any other heavenly body—in Flatland, it is impossible for us to tell North in the way you do. However, we have a method of our own.

By a Law of Nature in Flatland, there is a constant pull from the South. This pull is quite enough to serve as a compass in most parts of

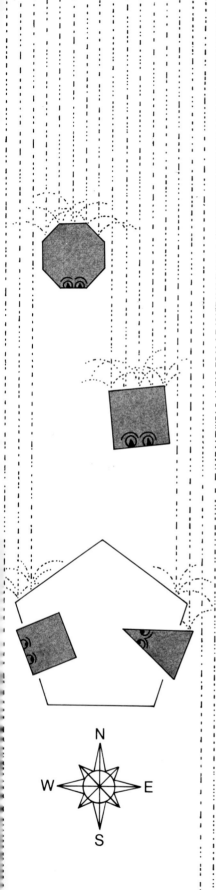

N

W ─ E

S

Flatland. Moreover, the rain, which falls at regular times each day, comes always from the North, so this is an additional help. And in the towns we have the help of the houses, for every house is built with the roof pointing North, to keep off the rain.

However, in our more northern regions, the pull of the South is hardly felt. Sometimes, when walking across an open plain where there have been no houses to guide me, I have had to stand and wait for hours until the rain came. Only then could I be sure of the direction in which I was going.

Our houses are quite comfortable and very well-suited to our climate and way of life. The most common form of house construction in Flatland is Five-Sided, or Pentagon-Shaped, as shown in the drawing.

The two northern sides make up the roof, and usually have no doors. On the East, there is the door by which we go in. On the West side, there is another door by which we go out. In this way, we are able to go in and out without bumping into and hurting one another. The south side, or floor, is usually doorless.

Square and Triangular houses are not allowed. There is a good reason for this. The angles of a Square (and still more of a Triangle) are much more pointed than the angles of a Pentagon. The lines of houses and almost all other objects are dimmer than the lines of Men and Women. Therefore,there is a danger that the points of a Square or Triangular house might do serious injury to an absent-minded traveler suddenly running against them.

As early as the eleventh-century of our era, Triangular houses were forbidden by law. The only exceptions were forts and similar kinds of buildings, where the sharp points might serve a useful purpose. At this period, Square houses were still permitted. But about three centuries later, the Law decided (for reasons of public safety) that in all towns with a population above ten thousand, the angle of the Pentagon was the smallest house angle that could be allowed. It is only now and then, in some very remote and backward farming district, that one may still discover a Square house.

We have no windows in our houses. This is because light comes to us both inside and outside, by day and by night, equally at all times and in all places. But where light comes from, we do not know. In the old days, our wise men liked to try to discover the cause of light, but this filled our hospitals with those who went mad trying to solve the problem.

I—alas, I alone in Flatland—know the true solution to this mysterious problem. But I cannot make my knowledge understandable to a single one of my countrymen. I am mocked at—I, the only one who knows the truth: that light comes from your strange world of three dimensions!

The book *Flatland* was written nearly one hundred years ago. You may find it a bit hard to read, but it is an interesting and often funny book that a good reader can enjoy. The author (whose real name was Edwin Abbott) tells how A. Square makes his way into the world of a Point, where there is no length, or width, or thickness. He also travels to Lineland, where there is only the one dimension of length. And he goes to our world—Spaceland—where he finds that there are the three dimensions of length, width, and thickness. But when A. Square tries to tell his fellow Flatlanders about these places, he is thrown into prison!

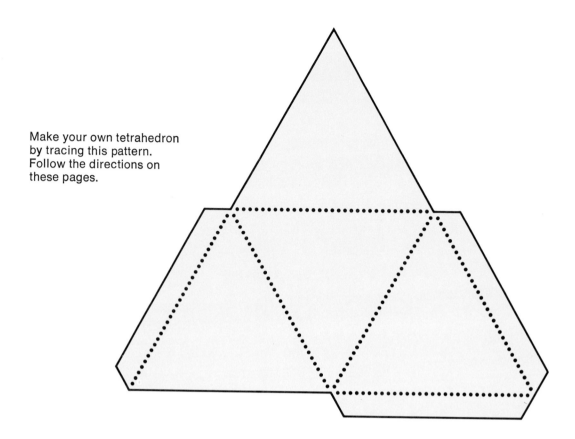

Make your own tetrahedron by tracing this pattern. Follow the directions on these pages.

Pyramids and other solid shapes

What's this? It looks like a design made out of triangles. Well, it is—but it's also something that you can make into something else!

Trace the design on a piece of paper and then cut it out. If you want to make a much stronger construction, you can glue your tracing on construction paper before you cut it out. Fold the paper on the dotted lines. Then open the paper and fold the flaps down.

Working with one flap at a time, put a bit of glue on each flap, then stick the flap to the

tetrahedrons

underside of the triangle next to it. You'll easily
be able to tell where the flaps go. When you've
done all this, you'll find that you have made a
sort of pyramid. A shape of this kind, with four
triangular sides that are exactly the same, is
called a tetrahedron (teht ruh HEE druhn).

A tetrahedron is what is called a solid shape.
It is a shape that has three dimensions—length,
width, and thickness. A flat shape, such as a
triangle, has only length and width. The piece
of paper you used is a flat shape. And the four
triangles on the paper are also flat shapes. Yet,
you made a solid shape. And the fact is, a great
many solid shapes can be made out of flat
shapes.

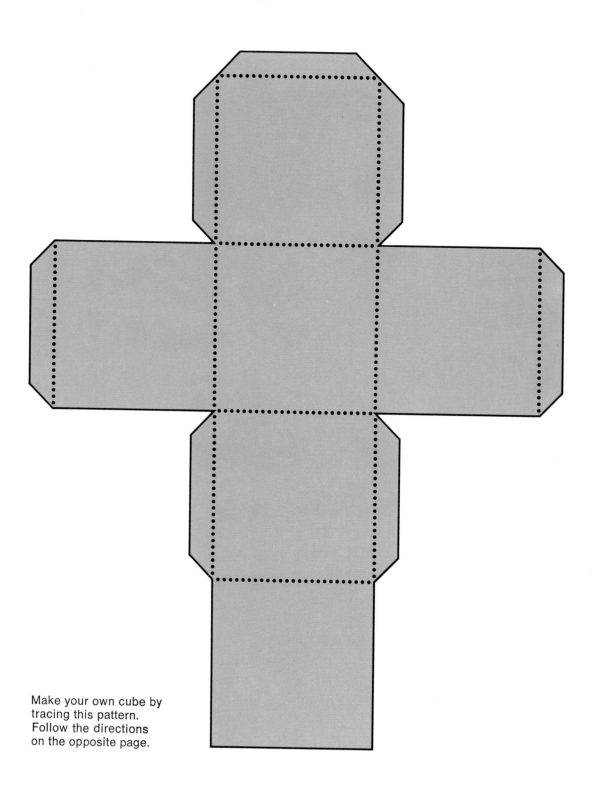

Make your own cube by
tracing this pattern.
Follow the directions
on the opposite page.

270

Long ago, in ancient Greece, a group of men who spent most of their time studying numbers and shapes discovered how to make many solid shapes out of flat shapes. Some of the things they discovered are surprising. You might have fun trying to make some of the things they did.

For example, these six squares will make a shape that you know quite well—a cube.

Cut out the shape and fold the paper on the dotted lines. Then glue each of the flaps to an underside of a square (once again, you'll easily be able to tell where the flaps go).

cubes

octahedrons

Here's another shape made of triangles. It's a little harder to make than the other two. But if you can do it, you'll find you've made a shape called an octahedron (ahk tuh HEE druhn), a shape that has eight flat faces, or sides.

The octahedron may look familiar to you. It looks like a diamond. And, as a matter of fact, real diamonds are often found in the shape of an octahedron.

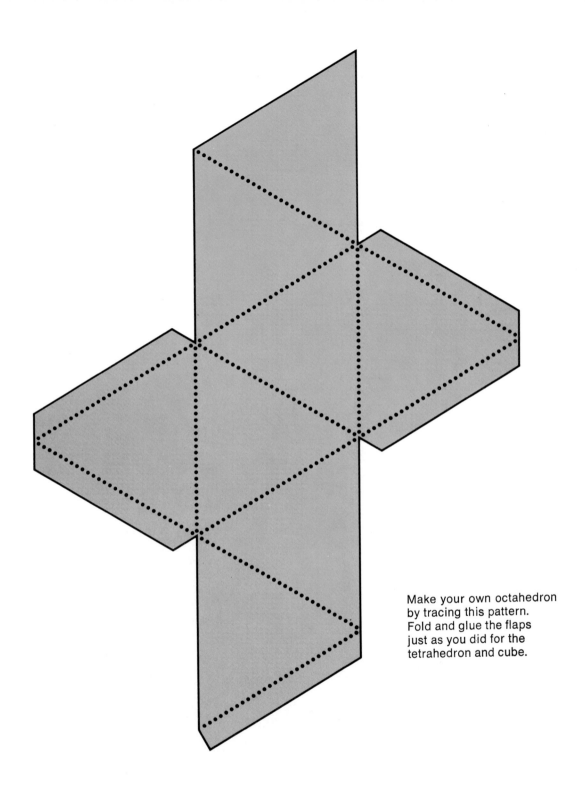

Make your own octahedron
by tracing this pattern.
Fold and glue the flaps
just as you did for the
tetrahedron and cube.

Here's a pattern for making still another solid shape out of triangles. It's even harder to make than an octahedron, but if you can make it, you'll have a shape with twenty equal sides—an icosahedron (eye koh suh HEE druhn).

icosahedrons

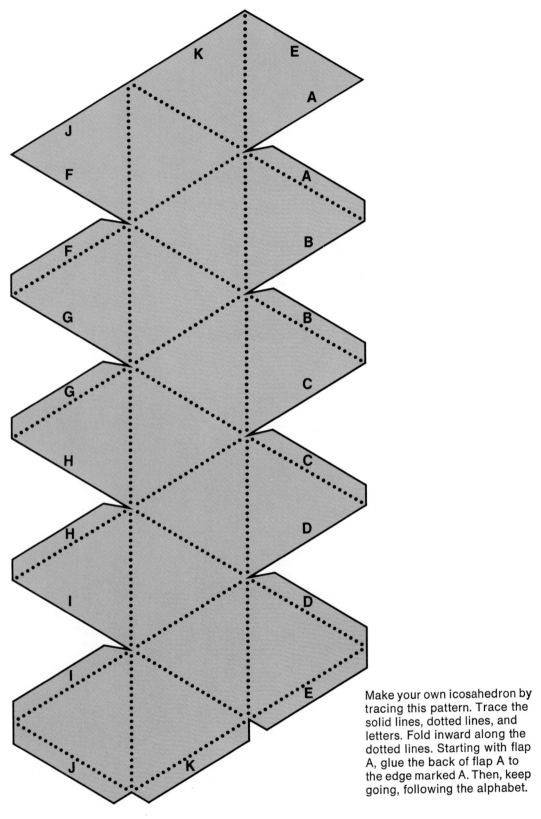

Make your own icosahedron by tracing this pattern. Trace the solid lines, dotted lines, and letters. Fold inward along the dotted lines. Starting with flap A, glue the back of flap A to the edge marked A. Then, keep going, following the alphabet.

Make your own dodecahedron by tracing this pattern. Trace the solid lines, dotted lines, and letters. Fold inward along the dotted lines. Starting with flap A, glue the back of flap A to the edge marked A. Then, keep going, following the alphabet.

276

dodecahedrons

This next shape is a little easier to make, but
still rather hard. It's made out of pentagons,
and it's called a dodecahedron (doh deh kuh
HEE druhn)—a solid shape with twelve sides.

The ancient Greeks who discovered how to make these shapes called them regular solids. A regular solid is a shape with an even number of sides that are all the same size and shape.

There are many other solid shapes that can be made out of flat shapes. But most of these solid shapes have an unequal number of sides or differently shaped sides. For example, the pyramids built by the Egyptians have five sides. Four of the sides are triangles, but the fifth side, the bottom, is a square.

You might find it fun to see just how many different kinds of solid shapes you can make out of flat ones. It's actually possible to make any kind of solid shape out of a flat one—even a ball! If you don't think so, look at a baseball. You'll see that two flat pieces of leather, cut to a special shape, were sewn together to cover the round ball!

The Transamerica building in San Francisco is a pyramid. Each side is a triangle and the bottom is a square.

Balls are solid shapes that can be made from such flat shapes as ovals and hexagons, as you can see from these balls.

Use the patterns in this book to make your own Christmas
tree ornaments. Cubes, pyramids, and other shapes can be
made of colored or painted paper. You can paint designs
on them, glue on beads, and decorate them in many ways.

8

People who work with numbers and shapes

The astronomer scans the depths of space
To find an unknown star.
But how will he know its distance?
Mathematics soon tells him how far!

The engineer plans a gleaming bridge,
To span a broad, blue bay.
He must figure out weight, and stress, and strain,
And mathematics shows him the way!

Engineers, scientists, and others, too,
Use math every day, as a rule.
For in the work these people do,
Mathematics is a valuable tool!

Solving problems

Far, far above the blue and white globe of the Earth, a strange machine, shaped much like a windmill, rushes out into the endless blackness of space. It is a space probe, sent from Earth to seek information about other planets. In a few months, the Earth will be only a bright point of light, far behind it.

Before a space probe such as this is sent out from Earth to travel to Mars, Venus, or another planet, many problems must be worked out.

A space vehicle must be launched at a certain speed to escape the pull of gravity. The vehicle has to follow a path that will take it to where another planet is *going to be*, not to where the planet *was* when the vehicle was launched. All these complicated problems of weight, speed, and direction are figured out by people who are mathematicians (math uh muh TISH uhnz).

Many people use mathematics in their daily work. But mathematics *is* the work of mathematicians.

Mathematicians worked out the complicated maze of wires and switches that easily handle thousands of telephone calls at the same time. And mathematicians put together much of the information that goes into computers. These computers then quickly work out problems that would take people months to solve.

Mathematicians are also teachers at colleges and universities. And some mathematicians simply *think* about mathematics and new ways to use numbers and shapes to solve problems.

Mathematicians helped to plan Skylab, a space vehicle in which astronauts lived and worked for months at a time.

Scientists called physicists use a lot of mathematics in their work. As you can see, they use letters and symbols more often than numbers.

Atoms, electrons, forces

On a desert in New Mexico, a large number of people crowded into a small, underground shelter made of thick concrete. Some distance away stood a tall, pointed tower made of steel girders. At the top of this tower was a little machine that was going to make history.

It was five-thirty in the morning, and dawn was just breaking over the desert. Suddenly, a tremendous flash lit up the desert for miles! The steel tower vanished in a puff of smoke! There was a terrible noise, like the loudest roar of thunder ever heard. A huge cloud of fire, six miles (9.6 kilometers) high, could be seen 180 miles (290 kilometers) away!

This happened a little more than thirty years ago. The people in the underground building had just exploded the first atomic bomb.

Many of the people who worked on the first atomic bomb were the kind of scientists called physicists (FIHZ uh sihsts). The science they work at is called physics (FIHZ ihks). Physics is the study of matter and energy. It is a way of finding out what makes nonliving things work.

Physicists study the behavior of atoms, out of which everything, from stars to people, is made. Physicists also study such things as motion, heat, and light, as well as forces such as gravity, electricity, and magnetism. The work and discoveries of physicists have helped give us such things as atomic energy, X rays, radio and television, refrigeration and air conditioning, and much, much more.

And much of the work of physicists—nearly all of it sometimes—is done with mathematics. However, the mathematics that physicists use isn't much like the arithmetic you're familiar with. Physicists seldom use numerals. They use letters and symbols that stand for ideas and forces. For example, the mathematical equation that showed physicists that they could release atomic energy looks like this: $E = mc^2$.

This equation may not look like much to you, but it led to the Atomic Age. Actually, this mathematical "sentence," or equation, says, "Energy [power] is equal to mass [an amount of material] multiplied by the speed of light squared." Perhaps you can't understand the equation—but a physicist can!

Physicists are scientists who use mathematics to study light, sound, and other things. From their work has come machines such as this one, called a laser, which can cut metal with a beam of light!

Costs, profits, losses

Suppose that one hot, summer afternoon you decide to go into business selling glasses of cool lemonade to thirsty people. It would be fun, of course, but you would probably also hope to make some money—a profit.

Accountants are people whose job is using arithmetic to keep track of the money that is made and spent by businesses, government, banks, and other organizations.

In order to start your lemonade business, there are some things you would need to know. First, how much should you charge for a glass of lemonade? Can you just make up a price?

In a real business, an accountant (uh KOWN tuhnt) helps to decide the prices of things, and figures out if a profit is being made. Most of an accountant's work is done with arithmetic.

If an accountant were to figure out things for your lemonade business, he or she would probably first find how much you will have to pay for the lemons and sugar, or the lemonade mix, that you'll need to make the lemonade. The cost of the material is one of the things you need to know to decide what the price of a glass of lemonade should be.

If it costs sixty cents to make just enough lemonade for ten glasses, the accountant might tell you to charge at least fifteen cents for a glass. That way, you need sell only four glasses to get back the cost of your materials—the sixty cents worth of lemons and sugar, or the lemonade mix. Every glass you sold after that would be profit.

If you sold all ten glasses, the accountant would tell you that you had made a *profit* of ninety cents! But if you sold only three glasses, the accountant would say that your business showed a *loss* of fifteen cents—because you didn't sell enough lemonade to get back the sixty cents the materials cost.

That's the sort of work accountants do. But in the world of big business, their work is much more complicated. They must often keep track of *millions* of dollars! A real business couldn't get along without an accountant.

Stars, comets, planets

The stars that twinkle in the sky at night are tremendously far away. Even the closest one, called Proxima Centauri (PRAHK suh muh sen TAWR eye), is some twenty-five million million miles (forty million million kilometers) away! No one could measure that great a distance. So how do we know how far away Proxima Centauri is?

Astronomers use mathematics to figure out the distances to stars and to work out star movements. This astronomer is inside a telescope that can take pictures of large parts of the sky.

We know because of the work of scientists called astronomers (uh STRAHN uh muhrs). The word *astronomer* means something like, "one who studies the ways of stars." Astronomers study stars, comets, planets, and everything else in space, to help us know as much as we can about the wonderful universe we're all part of. And to find out many things, astronomers use mathematics.

For example, to find the distance to a star, astronomers use the kind of mathematics called trigonometry (trihg uh NAHM uh tree), which means "triangle measurement." Trigonometry gives us a way to measure angles and find distances by figuring out triangles.

A triangle has three sides and three angles. If you know three parts of a triangle, one of which must be a side, you can figure out each of the other three parts. And, as you can see in the diagram, this is the way astronomers find the distance to a star.

Most things in space are so far away that astronomers don't usually measure distance in miles. They use light-years. A light-year is the distance light travels in one year.

Light moves at a speed of 186,282 miles (299,792 kilometers) a second. This means that in one year light travels 5.88 million million miles (9.46 million million kilometers). At this speed, light from Proxima Centauri takes 4.3 years to reach Earth. So an astronomer would say that this star is 4.3 light-years away.

Astronomers use mathematics for a great many other things, too, such as figuring out the sizes of things in space, the movements of stars and planets, and so on. Mathematics is a big part of an astronomer's job.

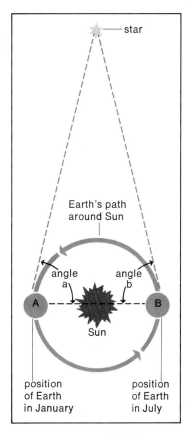

Astronomers know how far Earth is from the Sun, so they know one side of the triangle, the distance from A to B. Measuring angles a and b, they can figure out the distance to the star.

Bridges, mines, machines

A great, shining bridge across a broad river. A vehicle speeding through the cold darkness of space, toward another planet. A new kind of plastic, one that's tougher than steel. A giant electric power plant.

Before such marvelous things as these can come to be, someone has to think about them, plan how to make them, and solve the problems that come up. Who does all these things?

People called engineers (EHN juh nehrs) are the ones who plan and put together everything from new kinds of light bulbs to modern super highways a thousand miles long. Engineers also work on the planning and construction of buildings, the control of air pollution and water pollution, the design of ships, and a great many other things.

There are five main kinds of engineers. Civil

Much of the mathematics in planning buildings, bridges, and other things is done by computers. Even the shape of a building can be shown on a computer.

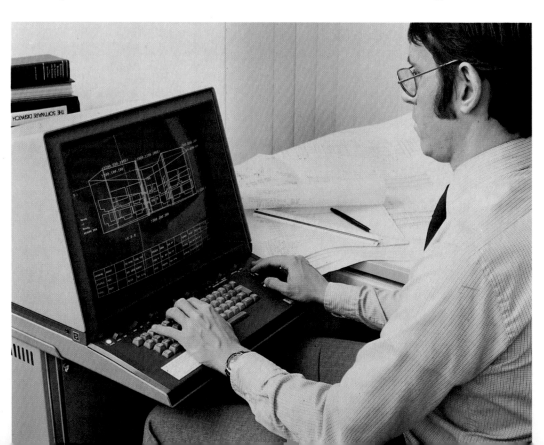

The Opera House in Sydney, Australia, is a marvel of mathematical shapes.

engineers plan and oversee the building of dams, bridges, roads, and similar things. Mechanical engineers plan and build such things as engines for automobiles and airplanes, and all the kinds of machines used in industry.

Chemical engineers create new products and materials out of the earth's resources. Mining engineers search for new sources of minerals, and plan and design ways of removing these minerals from the earth. Electrical engineers work on the production and use of electricity and design equipment that uses electricity.

Most engineers use a lot of mathematics in their work. A civil engineer building a bridge has to know how many tons of moving weight the bridge will hold. A chemical engineer may have to figure out just how much of a liquid will evaporate, and how quickly, when it is heated to a certain temperature. A mechanical engineer might have to work out the effects of vibration and heat on parts of an engine.

Engineers work with such things as shapes, measurements, weights, temperatures, and quantities of material—so mathematics plays a big, big part in most kinds of engineering.

Number facts

How would you like to be able to see into the future? If so, you should be a statistician (stat uh STIHSH uhn) when you grow up!

The word *statistician* means "a person who works with statistics (stuh TIHS tihks)." The word *statistics* simply means "number facts." And part of a statistician's job is to use number facts to "see" into the future!

How? Well, suppose your class is going to hold an election for class president. You could go to each person in the class and ask them whom they are going to vote for.

You might find that ten people plan to vote for Rick, seventeen for Kathy, and thirty-three for Jan. You'd be pretty sure that Jan would win. The numbers have shown you the future!

Asking questions of people is one way of gathering statistics. Of course, most of the work statisticians do is a great deal more complicated.

For example, a town might want to know if a new school is needed. A statistician could find out by gathering information on the number of children who will start school in coming years, the number of new families with children that may move into town, and so on. Working with these number facts, the statistician will be able to tell the community how many schoolrooms will be needed over the next few years.

Statisticians work with government, labor, business, industry, hospitals, laboratories, newspapers—in fact, just about everywhere! Their work is extremely important for all of us. Many of the things they find out about help us to make decisions about the things we do, buy, and use every day!

Statisticians are people who use numbers to plan for the future. The charts these statisticians are working with show how many people will be living in different parts of a city in years to come.

Books to Read

You may feel that the mathematics books you
use in school aren't much fun to read. But lots
of books about mathematics *are* fun to read!
They've been specially written and illustrated
to show you the real excitement and fun of
mathematics. Here are a few such books. You'll
find many other good ones in your public library.

Ages 5 to 8

Circles by Mindel and Harry Sitomer
(Crowell, 1971)
Can you draw a perfectly round circle? This book
will show you how. Do you know the different parts
of a circle? The book will tell you all about them.

Exploring Triangles: Paper Folding Geometry
by Jo Phillips (Crowell, 1975)
Colorful pictures show you how to fold paper to
make different kinds of triangles.

Fractions Are Parts of Things
by J. Richard Dennis (Crowell, 1971)
In this book, simple pictures and color are used
to show the parts of shapes and sets to help you
understand fractions.

How Did Numbers Begin? by Mindel and Harry
Sitomer (Crowell, 1976)
The story of how and why people first began to
use numbers.

Shapes by Jeanne Bendick
(Franklin Watts, 1968)
This book will help you see the many kinds of
shapes that are all around you. It also shows
you how to do experiments with shapes.

**Straight Lines, Parallel Lines, Perpendicular
Lines** by Mannis Charosh (Crowell, 1970)
With such things as pencil, paper, and string,
you can do experiments with all kinds of lines.

3D 2D 1D by David A. Adler (Crowell, 1975)
Lots of funny pictures help you to learn about
such things as length, area, and volume.

Ages 9 to 12

The Abacus: A Pocket Computer by Jesse Dilson
   (St. Martin's, 1968)
This book tells of the development of the abacus, its
history, and present-day use in China and Japan. Also
included is the story of an actual "race" between an
ancient abacus and a modern computer.

Arithmetic for Billy Goats by Donald Barr
   (Harcourt, 1966)
In this amusing book, an enterprising young goat,
William Gruff, invents a new system for counting corn
cobs. The system shows you examples of computer
arithmetic that are fun and easy to work out.

Math Menagerie by Robert R. Kadesh
   (Harper, 1970)
Here are twenty-five puzzles and projects that
will introduce you to such interesting fields of
mathematics as binary numbers, probability, and
soap-film geometry.

Sportsmath: How it Works by Lee Arthur, Elizabeth
   James, Judith B. Taylor (Lothrop, 1975)
If you like sports more than math, here's a book
that combines them both in an interesting way. It
shows you how arithmetic is used to get such
things as fielding and batting averages in baseball
and yards-per-pass attempt in football.

Symmetry by Arthur G. Razzell and K. G. O. Watts
   (Doubleday, 1968)
Symmetry means a balanced, or even, shape in
geometry. With puzzles, experiments, and diagrams,
this book shows symmetry in nature and mathematics.

Take Shapes, Lines, and Letters by Jeanne Bendick
   (McGraw, 1962)
This book shows the relationship of mathematics
to art, music, nature, secret codes, and many
other things that are likely to interest you.

Three and Shapes of Three by Arthur G. Razzell
   and K. G. O. Watts (Doubleday, 1969)
Here is the surprising story of the number three
and the part it has played in history, literature,
and mathematics. Fascinating problems with triangles
and polyhedrons are included.

New Words

Here are some of the words you have met in this book. Many of them may be new to you, but all of them are used in mathematics. Next to each word you'll see how to say the word: **acute** (uh KYOOT). The part shown in capital letters is said a little more loudly than the rest of the word. One or two sentences under each word tell what the word means.

acute (uh KYOOT)
Acute means sharp. An acute angle is any angle that is less than a right angle, thus forming a sharp shape.

avoirdupois (av uhr duh POYZ)
Avoirdupois means "goods of weight." Avoirdupois weight is a system of weight based on a 16-ounce pound.

capacity (kuh PAS uh tee)
Capacity is the amount of room inside a container, or the amount a container will hold.

cipher (SY fuhr)
In mathematics, a cipher is zero, any number, or any Arabic numeral. To cipher means to do arithmetic.

circumference (suhr KUHM fuhr uhns)
Circumference is the edge, as well as the distance around the edge, of a circle.

cone (kohn)
A cone is a solid shape that has a flat, round base and comes to a point at the top.

cube (kyoob)
A cube is a solid shape with six square sides, all equal.

cubic (KYOO bihk)
Cubic means shaped like a cube. A cubic number is the number you get by multiplying a number by itself twice, such as $2 \times 2 \times 2 = 8$.

cubit (KYOO biht)
A cubit was an ancient unit of length, about 18 to 22 inches. It was based on the length of the forearm, from the elbow to the tip of the middle finger.

cylinder (SIHL uhn duhr)
A cylinder is a solid shape formed by curving a rectangle so that its edges touch, forming circles of an equal size at each end. A hose is a cylinder.

decagon (DEHK uh gahn)
A decagon is a flat shape with ten sides and ten angles.

degree (dih GREE)
A degree is a unit of measurement. We measure temperature, angles, and any part of the curve of a circle in degrees. *See also* **unit.**

diameter (dy AM uh tuhr)
Diameter is the width of a circle—the distance through the center of a circle, from one edge to the other.

digit (DIHJ iht)
A digit is any numeral from 0 to 9. It is also a finger or toe.

dimension (duh MEHN shuhn)
Dimension is a measurement of length, width, or thickness.

dodecahedron (doh deh kuh HEE druhn)
A dodecahedron is a solid shape that has twelve sides.

equation (ih KWAY zhuhn)
An equation is a mathematical sentence that says two things are equal; $2 + 2 = 4$ is an equation.

equilateral (ee kwuh LAT uhr uhl)
Equilateral means "equal sides." An equilateral triangle is a flat shape with three equal sides.

gram (gram)
The gram is the basic unit of weight in the metric system. *See also* **metric system.**

heptagon (HEHP tuh gahn)
A heptagon is a flat shape with seven sides and seven angles.

hexagon (HEHK suh gahn)
A hexagon is a flat shape with six sides and six angles.

hypotenuse (hy PAHT uh noos)
The hypotenuse is the side of a right triangle opposite the right angle.

icosahedron (eye koh suh HEE druhn)
An icosahedron is a solid shape that has twenty sides.

irregular (ih REHG yuh luhr) **shape**
An irregular flat shape has unequal angles and sides of unequal length. An irregular solid shape has an uneven number of sides that are not the same size or shape. *See also* **regular shape.**

isosceles (eye SAHS uh leez)
Isosceles means "equal legs." An isosceles triangle is a flat shape that has two equal legs, or sides.

liter (LEE tuhr)
The liter is the basic unit of capacity in the metric system. *See also* **capacity; metric system.**

meter (MEE tuhr)
The meter is the basic unit of length in the metric system.

metric (MEHT rihk) **system**
The metric system is a system of weights and measures in which each unit of measurement is ten times larger than the next smallest unit. *See also* **gram; liter; meter.**

negative (NEHG uh tihv) **number**
A negative number is a number less than zero. Negative numbers are shown with a minus sign ($-$) in front of them. *See also* **positive number.**

nonogon (NAHN uh gahn)
A nonagon is a flat shape that has nine sides and nine angles.

numeral (NOO muhr uhl)
A numeral is a symbol, letter, or word that stands for a number.

obtuse (uhb TOOS)
Obtuse means blunt. An obtuse angle is any angle greater than a right angle, thus forming a blunt shape.

octagon (AHK tuh gahn)
An octagon is a flat shape that has eight sides and eight angles.

parallelogram (par uh LEHL uh gram)
A parallelogram is a four-sided, flat shape whose opposite side are equal and parallel (the same distance apart at all points).

pentagon (PEHNT uh gahn)
A pentagon is a flat shape that has five sides and five angles.

positive (PAHZ uh tihv) **number**
A positive number is a number that is more than zero. We count with positive numbers. *See also* **negative number.**

radius (RAY dee uhs)
A radius is a straight line from the center of a circle to any point on the edge (circumference) of a circle. It is also the distance from the center to the edge of a circle.

regular (REHG yuh luhr) **shape**
A regular flat shape has equal angles and sides of equal length. A regular solid shape has an even number of sides that are all the same size and shape. *See also* **irregular shape.**

scalene (skay LEEN)
Scalene means "uneven legs." The sides and angles of a scalene triangle are unequal.

sequence (SEE kwuhns)
Sequence means coming one after another. The numerals 2,4,6,8 form a number sequence.

tetrahedron (teht ruh HEE druhn)
A tetrahedron is a solid shape that has four sides.

unit (YOO niht)
A unit is a single thing. It is also an amount used to measure things. Seconds, minutes, and hours are units used to measure time.

Illustration Acknowledgments

The publishers of *Childcraft* gratefully acknowledge the courtesy of the following photographers, agencies, and organizations for illustrations in this volume. When all the illustrations for a sequence of pages are from a single source, the inclusive page numbers are given. In all other instances, the page numbers refer to facing pages, which are considered as a single unit or spread. All illustrations are the exclusive property of the publishers of *Childcraft* unless names are marked with an asterisk (*).

Cover: Aristocrat and Standard Binding—*Childcraft* photo
Heritage Binding—Kinuko Craft; *Childcraft* photo; George Suyeoka; Transamerica Corporation*; *Childcraft* photo; Kinuko Craft; *Childcraft* photos; Time Museum, Henrici's Clock Tower Inn, Rockford, Illinois (*Childcraft* photo)
1–3: *Childcraft* photo
8,9: *Childcraft* photo
10–15: George Suyeoka
16,17: *Childcraft* art; George Suyeoka
18–21: George Suyeoka
22,23: *Childcraft* photo
24,25: *Childcraft* art; Janet Palmer
26–45: Janet Palmer
46,47: *Childcraft* photo
48,49: Jean Helmer
50–53: Bill and Judie Anderson
54,55: Jean Helmer
56–59: Bill and Judie Anderson
60,61: Bill and Judie Anderson; *Childcraft* photo
62,63: *Childcraft* photo; Bill and Judie Anderson
64–69: Bill and Judie Anderson
70,71: Jean Helmer; *Childcraft* art
72,73: Bill and Judie Anderson; *Childcraft* art
74,75: Sue Snyder; Time Museum, Henrici's Clock Tower Inn, Rockford, Illinois (*Childcraft* photo); *Childcraft* art
76,77: University of Michigan Library*; Sue Snyder
78,79: *Childcraft* art
80–83: George Suyeoka
84,85: George Suyeoka; *Childcraft* art
86,87: George Suyeoka; Commodore Business Machines Inc.*; Merchandise National Bank of Chicago (*Childcraft* photo); *Childcraft* photo
88,89: *Childcraft* photo
90–93: Larry Ross
94–113: Kinuko Craft
114,115: Jenny Williams
116,117: Jenny Williams: Flexo Design
118,119: Jenny Williams
120,121: Kinuko Craft
122,123: Flexo Design; Kinuko Craft
124–127: Kinuko Craft
128,129: *Childcraft* art
130–133: Larry Ross
134–139: Jenny Williams
140–151: Larry Ross
152–155: Jean Helmer
156,157: Zorica Dabich; Willard K. Martin*
158–159: Jenny Williams
160,161: *Childcraft* photo
162–175: Dennis Hockerman
176,177: *Childcraft* photo
178,179: Bill and Judie Anderson
180,181: Kinuko Craft; American Numismatic Society*
182,183: The Louvre, Paris (*Childcraft* photo by Josse); Jack Wallen
184,185: Kinuko Craft
186–197: George Suyeoka
198,199: Bill and Judie Anderson
200,201: Kinuko Craft
202,203: The British Museum, London*; Robert Lackenbach, Black Star*; Bibliothèque Nationale, Paris*
204,205: Kinuko Craft

206,207: Time Museum, Henrici's Clock Tower Inn, Rockford, Illinois (*Childcraft* photo); Kinuko Craft
208,209: National Bureau of Standards*; Time Museum, Henrici's Clock Tower Inn, Rockford, Illinois (*Childcraft* photos)
210–213: Don Meighan
214,215: *Childcraft* photo; Don Meighan
216,217: *Childcraft* photo; Lietz*
218,219: Sue Snyder
220,221: *Childcraft* photo
222–231: George Suyeoka
232,233: *Childcraft* photo; *Childcraft* art
234–237: *Childcraft* art
238–247: George Suyeoka
248,249: *Childcraft* art; *Childcraft* photo
250,251: Wilbur Collection, Bailey Library University of Vermont*; *Childcraft* photo
252,253: *Childcraft* photo; Bill and Judie Anderson
254,255: George Gester, Photo Researchers*; *Childcraft* art
256,257: Donald Meighan
258–267: George Suyeoka
268–271: *Childcraft* art; *Childcraft* photo
272,273: *Childcraft* photo; *Childcraft* art
274–277: *Childcraft* art; *Childcraft* photo
278,279: Transamerica Corporation*; *Childcraft* photos
280,281: *Childcraft* photo
282,283: NASA
284,285: *Childcraft* photo; Korad
286,287: *Childcraft* photo
288,289: *Childcraft* photo; *Childcraft* art
290,291: Rob Chabot, DPI*; Skidmore, Owings and Merrill (*Childcraft* photo)
292,293: Northeastern Illinois Planning Commission (*Childcraft* photo)

Index

This index is an alphabetical list of the important things covered in both words and pictures in this book. The index shows you what page or pages each thing is on. For example, if you want to find out what the book tells about a particular subject, such as Arabic numerals, look under **Arabic numerals** or **numerals.** You will find a group of words, called an entry, like this: **Arabic numerals,** 76-77, *with pictures.* This entry tells you that you can read about Arabic numerals on pages 76 and 77. The words *with pictures* tell you that there are pictures of the Arabic numerals on these pages, too. Sometimes, the book only tells you about a thing and does not show a picture. Then, the words *with pictures* will not be in the entry. It will look like this: **acre** (unit of measurement), 191. Sometimes, there is *only* a picture of a thing in the book. Then the word *picture* will appear before the page number, like this: **laser** (tool), *picture,* 285.